Triathlon

Emotional Hurdles • Megachoice Marathon • Truth Relay

PrETEEN
ELECTIVES
AGES 10-12

A Curriculum for Preteens

STANDARD
PUBLISHING
Cincinnati, Ohio

Triathlon

About the Authors

Lynn Lusby Pratt's experience with upper elementary kids includes writing curriculum materials and teaching junior high Sunday school.

Debbie Allen is presently serving as a Children's Director. She has been in children's work for twelve of the eighteen years she has been in the ministry. The world expects fifth and sixth graders to act as adults and they want to be adults, but the reality is that they are still children. Debbie is committed to giving them every opportunity to be children.

Christine Spence has a bachelor's degree in education and journalism from Cincinnati Bible College and Seminary. She was a children's curriculum editor for seven years. She currently writes curriculum from her home.

Cover design and illustration by Brian Lovell and Anne Shaw
Inside illustrations by Anne Shaw/Sherry F. Willbrand

The Standard Publishing Company, Cincinnati, Ohio
A Division of Standex International Corporation
©1996 The Standard Publishing Company
All rights reserved
Printed in the United States of America

03 02 01 00 99 98 97 96   5 4 3 2 1
ISBN 0-7847-0502-X

Triathlon

Beyond childhood, heading to the next level, preteens struggle to find the right way. Help them handle their emotions, learn how to make right choices, and apply biblical truths at school. Help them learn the secrets to winning in real life!

Why "Next Level"?

Upper elementary kids—we'll call them preteens—are reaching, striving, groping toward the next level. They're in transition. They want to be taller, stronger, faster, and smarter as they catapult on their way to the next level.

In some ways preteens appear already to have arrived at the next level (once termed junior high). Preteens want to wear the right clothes, match hairstyles with athletes or rock stars, and fit in with the peer group no matter what! For many, however, the next level is an elusive goal: manly muscles and feminine curves are controlled by hormones not purchasing power.

So, too, the limits on thought structure. Many, if not most, fifth and sixth graders lack the ability to think critically, form logical arguments, or draw general principles from specific examples. There is usually a wide gulf between their level of experience and their ability to reflect on the meaning of their experiences.

Preteens are also still resolving the issue: *What can I do well?* rather than tackling the adolescent question: *Who am I?* So when preteens dress and act like their peers, they are striving for self-acceptance—feeling that they are as up-to-date as their peers, rather than endeavoring to establish a personal identity. Erickson's studies show that ten to twelve year olds are less involved with establishing a personal identity than they are with figuring out what they're really good at. This disparity creates difficulties for those using junior high curriculum for preteen classes: "What you see (a teenager) is not what you get (concrete-operational thinking and a different life task)."

Next Level curriculum is transitional: to help transitional preteens feel comfortable in teen-style learning settings and to equip leaders to teach within the limits of a preteen's limited development. Sessions are structured to help you teach preteens effectively in groups. The younger the student, the more discussion guidance must be given to identify appropriate conclusions and to suggest appropriate actions to be taken.

While many junior high topics are helpful and many elective curriculums look age appropriate, they often do not work with preteens because they were not designed for their limited thought processing and inexperienced discussion skills.

Next Level Preteen Electives! Planned and designed with preteen issues in mind and tailored for the learning capabilities of concrete thinkers! Visually appealing for the video generation. Emotionally satisfying for techno-driven kids.

This curriculum offers bonus opportunities for preteens to **Go to Extremes** serving others. It also strives to build family relationships—**Bridge the Gap**—during fun-filled family sessions.

So, because life is not a game—
pick a topic and recruit some helpers.
Start a group for ten to twelve year olds—
They'll be glad you did!

Next Level Preteen Electives address the importance of instilling values for character development.

This curriculum includes positive, choice-making strategies, friendship-making skills, care-giving and service skills, as well as refusal strategies (when appropriate). Each preteen in the program should feel accepted, important, and supported!

Surveys of Christian educators, Sunday school teachers, and Christian parents encourage us not to abandon the teaching of fundamentals. That's why Next Level curriculum includes units designed to equip kids to use the Bible, offers a survey of Bible heroes, and help kids fit in at church, among other topics. Future books will build mission awareness, encourage a strong sense of biblical stewardship, and help kids reconnect with adults who will guide them to maturity.

You can use Next Level Preteen Electives confidently, knowing that it is based on core biblical principles, permeated with Bible teaching, and presented in a way that ten to twelve year olds can understand and enjoy!

How are Next Level units organized?

Get Into the Game

As an introduction to the session, this section offers activities to grab the students' attention and encourage participation from the entire group.

These lesson steps offer activity choices that may be set up as learning centers or used as options. Depending on the class size, the teacher may divide the class into small groups. Each works on an activity. For this to be effective, ample assistance is needed.

If the class is small, the teacher can customize the session to fit that need. Select one or two options to utilize or have the class work together instead of dividing into small groups.

Step 1

Each activity is designed to help students dig deeper into the topic. A biblical study is always included in this section.

Step 2

This section offers another way to discover biblical truth.

Step 3

This activity involves the entire class to help students apply what was learned in Steps 1 and 2.

Take It to the Next Level

This final section concludes the session by helping students commit the principles they have learned to their own lives. The question, "So what does this mean to me personally?" can be answered in this section.

Extra Helps

Each unit introduction includes devotion suggestions for either the teacher and/or the students. The devotional ideas correlate with the sessions contained in that particular unit.

Reproducible pages are provided for your convenience. Photocopy these pages for your personal use or for your student's use to enhance each session.

Additional Resources

The following list of books, videos, and music serve as extra resources for each unit. Feel free to use these materials as research prior to teaching or as extra activities if you deem appropriate.

Unit 1—Emotional Hurdles

Kids in Danger (Training Your Child to Tame the Destructive Power of Anger) by Ross Campbell, M.D., Victor Books

Managing Your Emotions by Erwin Lutzer, Victor Books

Make Anger Your Ally by Neil Clark Warren, Ph.D., Focus on the Family Publishing

Helping Children Grieve (When Someone They Love Dies) by Theresa Huntley, Augsburg Fortress

The Spirit-Controlled Temperament by Tim LaHaye, Tyndale House Publishers, Inc.

Why You Act the Way You Do by Tim LaHaye, Tyndale House Publishers, Inc.

"Cry for Love" by Michael W. Smith (Reunion Records)

"Lovely Day" by Out of Eden (Gotee Records)

Unit 2—Megachoice Marathon

Teaching Your Kids the Truth About Consequences (Helping Them Make the Connection Between Choices & Results) by Dr. Daniel Hahn, Bethany House Publishers

"I Still Believe" by Church of Rhythm (Reunion Records)

Unit 3—Truth Relay

The Amazing Story of Creation From Science and the Bible by Duane T. Gish, The Institute for Creation Research.

Dinosaurs by Design by Duane T. Gish, Creation-Life Publishers

Discovering the Four Seasons by Jeffery Scott Wallace, Lion Publishing

Discovering Oceans, Lakes, Ponds, and Puddles by Jeron Ashford Frame, Lion Publishing

The Wonder of God's World, Air, Light, Water by Bonita Searles-Barnes, Lion Publishing

Faith Training—Raising Kids Who Love the Lord by Joe White, Ed.D., Focus on the Family Publishing

A Children's Companion Guide to America's History by
   Catherine Millard, Horizon House Publishers

*Pocahontas—The True Story of an American Hero and Her
   Christian Faith* by Andy Holmes, Educational Publishing
   Concepts

   "Evolution . . . Redefined" by Geoff Moore & the Distance
(Forefront)

   "I'm Not Ashamed" by Newsboys (Star Song)

   "The Evidence of God" by Geoff Moore & the Distance
(Forefront)

Emotional Hurdles

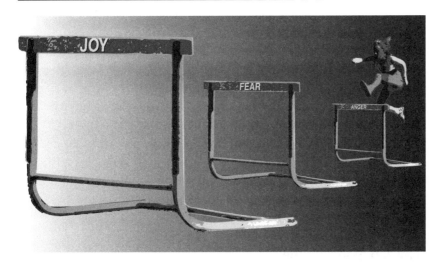

This unit is designed to bring your preteens to a new level of understanding about their emotions. The biblical perspective of each session will help them **Know** more and **Feel** better about themselves. Upon completion of this unit, students should be challenged to **Do** what God wants them to do in any situation—rather than to act on their own (often unreliable) emotions.

Developmental Appropriateness

"A person who does not control himself is like a city whose walls have been broken down" (Proverbs 25:28, *ICB).*

With divorce and crime rates on the rise, today's preteens are feeling especially insecure. What a perfect opportunity to help them build their lives on the only unshakable foundation!

Behavior characteristics related to preteen emotions:

1. Cyclical reactions, because their feelings go up and down.

2. Unreliable impressions, because emotions are unstable.

3. Demand independence, yet still are very dependent in many ways.

4. Mental confusion—debating whether or not to accept their parents' beliefs or voice their own opinions.

(Based on information from James Dobson's *Preparing for Adolescence.*)

Physical, mental, social, and emotional maturity will be different among the students in your group—not to mention different in *each* student. For example, the tallest boy may be the shyest. An emotionally mature girl may be immature physically.

Students this age like challenges, and they like the chance to make their own choices. However, they need tools to help them make good choices. **Emotional Hurdles** will equip them to make these choices.

Tips for Using These Sessions

1. A memory verse is suggested for each session. However, many helpful Scriptures are included in each session. If you think another verse might be more appropriate as a memory verse for your class, feel free to use it.

2. Because fifth and sixth graders will not do well sitting and writing for an hour, many of the activity options involve movement.

3. Step 1 in each session is a Cameo Appearance that gives a brief description of a famous Bible hero. Please note that these sessions are not designed to be built around specific characters. The cameo appearance simply gives the students a real person in Bible history with whom they can associate the theme of that particular session.

4. Students are encouraged to make "My Mood Manual" during the **Take It to the Next Level** section. This activity will encourage students to record specific situations or emotions they have experienced that relate to the day's topic. The students will then have an opportunity to pray about their emotions during the closing moments of the session.

To enhance the prayer time, obtain a "mood" tape. (These often feature streams, wind, birds, flute, etc.) Give attention to lighting, either dimming the lights or using candles.

You will find that your students rarely have a quiet moment. Some silence toward spiritual and emotional preparation will make these closing moments effective. Remember, meditation originated in the mind of God.

Video Clips

Video clips are suggested at the end of each session. These clips (from the ones suggested or others you think of) could be used as the students enter the room to reinforce one of the activities. Even a thirty to sixty second clip can be quite effective. (Suggested use of a video clip does not indicate endorsement of the movie.)

Devotional Thoughts

We might question whether Jesus experienced typical human emotions, especially in light of the way Jesus is often portrayed in movies: moving slowly and deliberately, little change in voice tone or facial expression. In general, He is often portrayed as an unresponsive, unemotional individual. But let's look again. The life of Jesus from the book of Mark will be the basis for this month's devotions.

Four selections are given, one for each week. However, we recommend you read the entire book of Mark.

Session 1—Mark 3:1-6; 9:14-26. Two healing miracles.
Session 2—Mark 4:35-41. Jesus calms the storm.
Session 3—Mark 11:1-25. The triumphal entry, cursing of the fig tree, and cleansing the temple.
Session 4—Mark 14:32-42 (compare with Psalm 22). Leading up to the crucifixion.

For maximum effect, use a notebook. Divide the pages into four columns: Scripture, What's Happening, Probable Emotion/Response, What Jesus Did.

As you read, note what's happening that would evoke an emotion or response. In the next column, list feelings Jesus probably had in response to those events: sadness, anger, sympathy, impatience. Then in the last column, note what Jesus actually did.

You will find it interesting that Jesus did not avoid confrontation. He usually responded with words—but not in uncontrolled, emotional outbursts. Then He invariably went ahead and did the right thing, regardless of what others thought or said.

What a fabulous example He is!

Scripture	What's Happening	Probable Emotion/Response	What Jesus Did

Session 1

Me, Myself, and I (Body and Soul)

Memory Verse. Proverbs 23:19

Know that God created us as complex, unique individuals.
Feel secure that we can communicate with God, who knows what's best.
Do what God wants—no matter how we feel.

Get Into the Game

Select one of the following activities to introduce today's topic.

Activity #1—Brain in a Jar

Allow each student to make a brain out of clay, drop it into his jar, and close the lid.

Then say, "God designed us to be complex individuals. We have a body, we have a brain, we have emotions, and we have a spirit, right? We have a connection with God.

"But sometimes our whole self doesn't work together as it should. Sometimes our emotions, our feelings, get our bodies into trouble because our brains forget to check in with God.

"Did any of you do anything silly or stupid this week? Did you leave your brain in a jar?" Share an experience of your own and allow willing students to contribute. Comment on the stories that involve emotions. You might say, "Doug was so angry that he left his brain in a jar and hit his little brother. Mary was so excited that she forgot to watch where she was going and fell off the porch."

Conclude this option by saying, "We want to understand ourselves. We need to learn how to let God help us with our decisions so we don't leave our brains in a jar. That's what we're talking about today."

Materials
modeling clay and a small jar for each student

Activity #2—Dress Up

Provide a wide assortment of clothing items (i.e., WW II army jacket, 1970s wooden cross necklace, Bible costume, Japanese kimono, Mexican serape). Allow each student to choose one item and put it on.

Comment on the dates of the clothing and the countries they represent. Let students divide into a "cool" side and a "dorky" side—depending on whether or not they'd wear this item to school.

Materials
items of clothing from different eras and countries

Say to the students, "We have definite ideas of what we want to wear, don't we? That's because fashion changes. Some of these clothes you labeled 'dorky' are worn today in other parts of the world. Some of the older clothes are funny now, but in their day, everybody wore them. They were 'in.'

"But did you know feelings don't go in and out of style? No matter where in the world we go and no matter if we go back thousands of years in history, we can't find any new emotions. Everybody experiences anger, sadness, happiness, and fear.

"God created us—and that includes our feelings. That's what we're going to talk about today."

Step 1

Distribute Bibles to students who did not bring their own. Then say: "Today our Bible character is the apostle Paul. What do you know about Paul?" Let the students create a simple profile. (*Paul wrote much of the New Testament; he fought against Christians before he became one; he was a preacher; he traveled a lot.*)

Materials
Bibles

Tell the students, "Paul is one of our great Bible heroes. But he was like us. Sometimes he had trouble getting his brain, his body, his feelings, and his spiritual side to work together. Let's see what he says."

Call on a student to read Romans 7:15. The *International Children's Bible* reads: "I do not understand the things I do. I do not do the good things I want to do. And I do the bad things I hate to do."

Say, "I can relate to that, can't you? I think Paul's secret to success was that he didn't trust his feelings. He stayed in touch with God, and let God lead him."

Step 2

(Note to teacher: Read the following Scriptures for your own study, then check the ones you want to emphasize in class. For this topic, we recommend the *International Children's Bible* for use with your students.)

Materials
Bibles

The suggested Scriptures are: Psalm 119:9, 10; Proverbs 14:30; 16:6; Romans 6:13, 19; 1 Corinthians 6:19, 20; 2 Corinthians 4:16; Philippians 2:13. The teacher comments in class should be adapted according to the Scriptures that are used. However, comments should resemble the following.

"Any time we talk about today's topic, we run into a problem. On the one hand, we learn that we are all unique, special, different, and full of emotions. On the other hand, we learn that we all are supposed to obey the same rules God has given.

So who, or what do we trust—feelings, teachers, parents, friends, or God?

"Well, a teacher may give you wrong advice; a parent's advice may even be off track (but don't tell your parents I said so!); your friends may sympathize with your problems, but they don't have the experience to know what's best. But God gives only good advice. He knows what's best. After all, He made us! He knows how we function. We are free to be ourselves, to be unique; yet God's rules can still apply to all of us without squelching our individual personalities.

"When we learn what God wants for us by studying His Word, we can grow in Him and become more confident. When we stay in communication with Him through prayer, then He will help us make wise decisions based on His truth instead of foolish ones based on our emotions."

Step 3

Select one of the following activities to help your students apply what they have learned. Use both options if you have time to do so.

Materials
paper and pencils and/or chalk and chalkboard

Activity #1—No More Talk Shows!

To introduce this option in a fun way, pretend to be an announcer. Say, "Ladies and Gentlemen, Channel 6 regrets to announce that all talk shows have been canceled today. All guests who were scheduled to appear have decided to do what God wants instead of being ruled by their feelings. So, you see, . . . well . . . now there's nothing to talk about."

Then become yourself again and continue. "Have you ever watched a talk show and thought, 'You know, if those people had done what God wanted in the first place, this whole mess would never have happened?' Let's think about this for a minute."

Ask students to name some recent talk show topics. You'll probably be surprised at how much they know, but have a few in mind, just in case they can't think of any. Use the chalkboard or paper and pencils and use these headings: What was the topic or situation? What was the person(s) feeling? How did the person(s) solve the problem? What would be God's desire in this situation? Work through several scenarios as time allows.

Say the following to close this activity. "I think we can see that the people on these shows who insist on doing what they want usually seem very unhappy. And they usually make lots of other people miserable, too! God's rules will help us control our emotions so problems will truly work out for the best."

Activity #2—Don't Leave Home Without It!

Let the students start coloring their mini posters as you talk. If you used Activity #1—Brain in a Jar during **Get Into the Game,** you have a natural lead-in to this option. If not, draw comments from that section as background for this poster. Read the memory verse together several times. Encourage the students to hang their posters in their rooms. Offer to give them extra copies if they want to give one to a friend.

Materials
photocopies of page 16, colored pencils or fine point markers

Take It to the Next Level

Distribute a photocopy of "My Mood Manual" to each student. Have each student cut the page into the four separate sections. Students may use pieces of construction paper as a cover for their pages. After students cut the paper, have them put the pages in order and staple the pages along the side to create a book. Have students write on their covers, _____ 's Mood Manual. Allow students to decorate their books.

Next, ask students to turn to the page that says, "Week 1." Ask the students to write down a time when their emotions may have gotten the best of them. What happened? While the mood tape is playing, have students finish writing in their manuals.

Dim the lights, if possible, or light a candle. Then have the students bow their heads, close their eyes, and remain silent for a minute. Read Psalm 139:23, 24 from the *International Children's Bible* as the prayer. "God, examine me and know my heart. Test me and know my thoughts. See if there is any bad thing in me. Lead me in the way you set long ago."

Materials
photocopies of page 17, construction paper, pencils, colored pencils or markers, scissors, stapler, mood tape, candle, Bible

Video Clips

Annie. The early scene at the orphanage (through the song "It's a Hard Knock Life") shows numerous feelings in action.

Your Brain

Don't Leave Home Without It!

"Keep your mind on what is right" (Proverbs 23:19, ICB).

My Mood Manual

Week 1

My Mood Manual

Week 2

My Mood Manual

Week 3

My Mood Manual

Week 4

Feelings (The Big Picture)

Memory Verse. Philippians 4:4

Know that it's normal to have a wide range of emotions.
Feel an association with the emotions of great Bible characters.
Plan a strategy to help remain calm in the midst of emotional storms.

Get Into the Game

Activity #1—My Life Is Ruined!

Without taking too much time, allow the students to construct the tower and begin play by taking turns removing pieces until the tower collapses.

After the game ends, discuss the different feelings involved in playing the game. There was probably excitement, happiness, irritation (if someone was pushing or endangering the tower), and worry (over not wanting to be the one to topple the tower).

Say to the students, "We all have a wide range of emotions that God gave us. Sometimes we feel on top of the world. And sometimes we feel as if our lives are ruined. Do you think it's possible to be happy even when something bad is happening? Can you be calm in the middle of something scary? Today, we're going to find out."

Materials
Jenga game or any similar tower building toy

Activity #2—Ups and Downs

Instruct one student to hold the one-minute timer. Another student holds the small bell, and one student is the contestant. The contestant must talk nonstop for one minute about a person he knows very well, such as a friend or relative. The catch is that, periodically and frequently, the bell will ring. The contestant begins by saying only good things. But when the bell rings, he must switch immediately (even if in mid-sentence), to saying only bad things. When the bell rings again, he switches back to saying good things again.

You or an outgoing, talkative student should go first. Allow two or three tries at this activity.

Then say, "It's quite a workout, isn't it, to jump immediately from good to bad and back again? You know, our feelings act just like that sometimes, don't they? We're on top of the world one minute. Then something happens, and we don't think

Materials
small bell, one-minute timer

we'll ever be happy again. Today we'll talk about our up and down feelings. They're normal, but let's see if the Lord can help us handle them a little better."

Step 1

Say, "Our Bible character making a brief appearance today is David. Who can tell me something about David?" Let the students respond. *(He was a shepherd, a musician, and a poet. He killed Goliath. He became king, stole another man's wife, and arranged for the man to be killed.)*

Say, "I'd say David's life was filled with ups and downs. David wrote most of the psalms in the Bible. Let's look at a couple of verses."

Call on two students to read the following two passages aloud.

Psalm 13:1, 2 (ICB): "How long will you forget me, Lord? How long will you hide from me? Forever? How long must I worry? How long must I feel sad in my heart? How long will my enemy win over me?"

Psalm 27:1 (ICB): "The Lord is my light and the one who saves me. I fear no one. The Lord protects my life. I am afraid of no one."

After the Scriptures have been read, say, "Wow! Can the same David have written both of those? Yes! Just like us, he had times when he was in the pits and times when he felt confident and happy. David is one of our great Bible heroes—not because he didn't have any troubles, but because he let God help him through them."

Materials
Bibles

Step 2

Before class, cut off the bottom Scripture (Philippians 4:4-7) from the photocopies. This will be used later in the session. Distribute the "Highs and Lows" portion. Assign students to read the different Scriptures aloud. (The Scriptures are Psalm 34:18; Psalm 81:1; Psalm 94:18, 19; Psalm 118:24; John 16:33.)

Then say, "Did you notice how these verses talk about both ups and downs, hope and joy, as well as sadness and burdens? The Bible is a very honest book.

"Our ups and downs might make us think of a roller coaster. We don't worry about the low points in the ride, because we're excited about the next peak. Maybe that's the lesson we can get from these Scriptures: Life does have low points. But if we're traveling with God, it's an exciting adventure.

"To help us remember this, we're going to put some of these verses onto our roller coaster art."

Materials
Bibles, photocopies of page 22, pencils

Of the verses read, allow students to choose whichever ones they want to use. They will write these along the roller coaster, arranging the words to suit the ups and downs of the art. For example, use John 16:33 (ICB): "In this world you will have trouble," would be written in a low spot; the rest of the verse, "But be brave! I have defeated the world!" would climb back up.

Step 3

Select one of the following activities to help your students apply what they have learned. Use both options if you have time to do so.

Activity #1—Three Rights

Arrange the cards on your class table or on a wall, in random order. Ask the class to work together to arrange the words in the best sentence. There will probably be some arguing. Listen to their reasons for their decisions.

When the students have finished, say, "If we put 'feel right' at the beginning, we have a problem. It's hard to control how we feel. We can't help 'feeling' angry or sad. But we can control our thinking. 'If you think right' by remembering what God has told us in some of our Scriptures today and 'act right' by doing what He says, no matter what, then He will change our feelings and 'you will feel right.'"

You can discuss this more, as time allows. Allow the students to write this sentence on the back of their reproducible pages. Encourage them to remember this formula during their next crisis.

Activity #2—The God Chunk

Supply each student with a pair of scissors and a sheet of construction paper.

Tell the students, "Cut out a shape, any kind of shape you want. Use as much of the sheet as you can—make it big!"

When they've finished, quickly remove the scraps and scissors. Say, "We're going to call these shapes our God chunks. We're going to say that each of us has, inside somewhere, a hole that fits exactly the cutout shape. Imagine that nothing has ever quite filled that hole the way I'd like. That's because it's a hole—an emptiness—that only God and His joy can fill."

Then give the students copies of the Philippians 4:4-7 passage you have made from the reproducible page. Supply glue or tape.

Tell the students, "We're going to fasten the Scripture from Philippians onto our God chunks. These can remind us to be

| IF YOU |
| THINK RIGHT |
| AND |
| ACT RIGHT |
| YOU WILL |
| FEEL RIGHT |

Materials
cards prepared using 5-by-7-inch or larger paper

Materials
photocopies of Scripture cut from page 22, construction paper, scissors, glue or tape

full of God's joy. If we are full of God's joy, it's as if we can see a bigger picture. Even when something bad happens, we don't have to be overcome by it. If we remember that we have God, we can know joy, even in the middle of rough times. We don't have to be empty. God's joy can help us be calm in the middle of life's storms."

Take It to the Next Level

Materials
"My Mood Manuals," pencils, Bible, mood tape, candle

Have the students turn to Week 2 in their manuals. Ask the students to complete the following statement: "The next time something happens that bothers me, I can . . ." Play the mood tape as students complete the sentence.

When the students have finished, dim the lights and allow a minute of complete silence to prepare the class for the closing prayer.

Pray this prayer, which has been personalized from 1 Thessalonians 5:16-18: "Lord, help us to always be happy. Help us to never stop praying. Help us to give thanks, no matter what happens. We know this is what You want for us."

Video Clips

Raiders of the Lost Ark. To show how quickly we can go from joy to despair, use the opening scene where Indiana Jones outruns the big boulder and escapes with the treasured idol only to land facing his arch enemy.

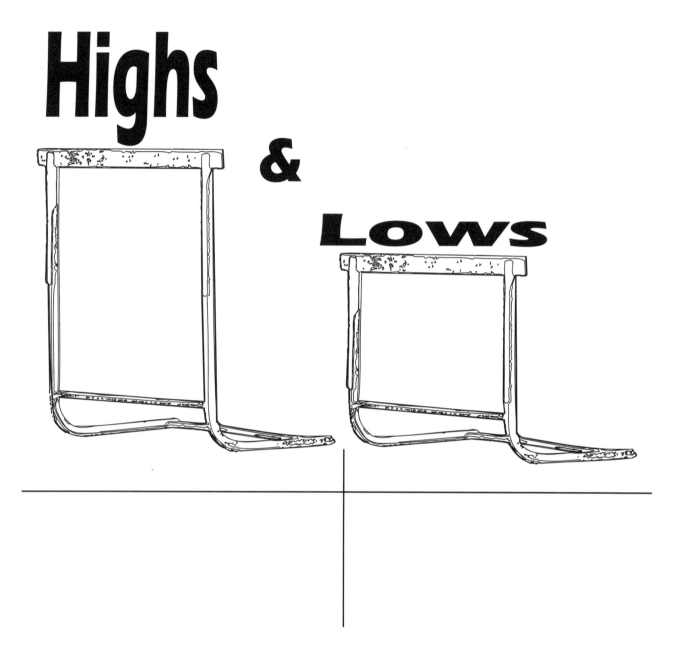

Highs & Lows

Find the following verses in your Bible. Write the Scriptures or portions of Scriptures that mention happy or positive situations under the "high" hurdle. Write those Scriptures that discuss troubles or negative situations under the "low" hurdle.

Psalm 34:18 • Psalm 81:1 • Psalm 94:18, 19 • Psalm 118:24 • John 16:33

"Be full of joy in the Lord always. . . . Do not worry about anything. But pray and ask God for everything you need. . . . The peace that God gives is so great that we cannot understand it" (Philippians 4:4-7, *ICB).*

Anger (Forgiveness vs. Revenge)

Memory Verse. Proverbs 15:1

Know that anger is a legitimate emotion.
Feel relieved that we don't have to act on
anger in destructive ways.
Promise to forgive one person.

Get Into the Game

Select one of the following activities to introduce today's topic.

*Activity #1—*I'm So Mad

Have the entire class, including yourself, stand in a circle.
Leave plenty of room to move around.

Tell the students, "We're going to play a little game about
anger. The person to my left will go first. We'll move around
the circle, and I'll be last. Everyone is to complete this sentence: 'I'm so mad I could . . .' When you fill in the word, we
will all act it out together. But when it's your turn, you must say
all the words from the beginning, in order, before adding your
new word. We will only act out the new word each time."
(Example: The first student says "I'm so mad I could scream,"
and everyone screams. The second student says, "I'm so mad I
could scream and cry," and everyone cries. The third student
says, "I'm so mad I could scream and cry and roll on the floor,"
so everyone rolls on the floor.)

When play gets back to you say, "Before I do mine, let's all
repeat the whole thing together, acting it out as we go." Have
everyone do this then say, "OK, it's my turn. Let's see, I'm so
mad I could scream and cry . . ." Finish the rest of the words,
then say, "And I'm so mad I could forgive."

Play should screech to a halt here. Ask the students to help
you come up with an action to represent *forgiving.* Ask why no
one thought of forgiving as a response to anger.

Lead into today's Scripture study by saying, "I think we've
seen that we're pretty good at being angry. But maybe we need
to know more about what God wants us to do with anger."

Activity #2—What Makes You Angry?

Place several items on the table. You might include: a $1 bill, local sports headline, a dish towel, a CD, a fast food bag and/or others. Then ask the students if any of these items make them angry. Do the items remind the students of incidents that upset them?

Pick up the $1 bill and say, "If you loaned money to your friend, but she keeps forgetting to pay you back, do you get angry every time you see money? Do you get angry when you see the friend or when you see your friend spending money?"

Continue with this illustration, showing possible associations with the items and anger. Some suggestions include:

1. local sports headline (My team would've won if they hadn't cheated.)

2. dish towel (Mom punished me by making me do the dishes for a week.)

3. CD (I've lost my favorite one. I've looked everywhere, but I can't find it.)

4. fast food bag (We ate there yesterday because everybody wanted to, except me.)

You can elaborate on this option by sharing an experience of your own or allowing a few students to share. Then say, "Different things make different people angry, don't they? Usually we get angry when we feel we've been hurt or treated unfairly. We're going to learn more about anger today."

Materials
various items such as a $1 bill, local sports headline from newspaper, dish towel, CD, fast food bag

Step 1

Say to the students, "The Bible character making a cameo appearance today is Joseph. Since we're talking about anger today, let's name some things that happened to Joseph that probably made him angry."

Help the students list these low points in Joseph's life:

1. His brothers threw him in a pit.

2. His brothers sold him.

3. He was carted off to a foreign country.

4. He was falsely accused.

5. He was thrown into prison.

6. The king's cup bearer promised to help him get out of prison, but he didn't.

Say to the students, "Joseph's troubles all started with his brothers. Do you think he ever hated them? Do you think he wanted to get even? How would you have felt?"

Let students respond, then say, "I'm sure Joseph had normal, angry feelings, just as we would have. But it seems that Joseph always tried to do what God wanted. Does anyone remember how the story ended?"

Materials
Bibles

Anger

Help students finish the story: Joseph ended up being a powerful man in Egypt. When he met his brothers years later, he could easily have gotten even with them. He did make them squirm a little, but in the end, he forgave them. His statement in Genesis 50:20 is classic, "You meant to hurt me. But God turned your evil into good" (ICB).

Step 2

Give each student a copy of "The Things We Say," a Bible, and a pencil. Let them work for a few moments, looking up the Scriptures and matching them to the numbered phrases. Although some Scriptures answer more than one saying, the intended matches are: 1-C, 2-A, 3-B, 4-F, 5-E, 6-D.

Use the completed worksheet as the basis for discussion on the topic of anger.

Be sure and make the point that the Bible tells us exactly how to deal with anger. Point out the difference between the way we usually respond to anger and the way the Bible suggests we respond.

Close this option by saying, "God understands our anger. He knows people sometimes do terrible things to each other. Our Scriptures even mentioned 'evil' and 'evil people,' didn't they? The Scriptures don't make any distinction between a little thing we might be angry about and a truly terrible thing that may have happened. God's response for dealing with anger is the same."

Materials
photocopies of page 27, pencils, Bibles

Step 3

Select one of the following activities to help your students apply what they have learned. Use both activities if you have time to do so.

Activity #1—Snake in a Can

Tell the students, "We've learned a lot about anger today. Maybe our snake in a can here can help us out, too."

Begin to stuff the snake in the can as you continue. "Some of you may be *stuffers* when it comes to anger. You just boil inside or get mad and cry in your room, but you don't really show it. Probably about half of us are like that. Which of you are anger stuffers?" Hopefully, some of the students will fess up. "Then the rest of us are probably *exploders*. You know what's going to happen when I open this can, don't you?" Open the can and let the snake pop out. "We exploders blow up when we're angry—and people had better get out of the way. Are there any exploders here?"

Materials
"snake-in-a-can" type of toy, chalkboard

Continue playing with the snake, if you wish, as you write the words *stuffers* and *exploders* on the chalkboard. Let the group come up with their own solutions to their problems of stuffing anger inside or exploding with anger. Help them list some more practical (and biblical) ways to handle their anger. Some examples:

1. Stuffers—talk to the person they're angry with; talk to a parent or friend about their hurt; pray for the other person; give themselves a time limit for pouting.

2. Exploders—count to ten; stop and decide if what happened is really worth getting mad over; try to speak calmly.

Activity #2—Betcha!

Let students answer the questions (bottom of page 27). Keep these few moments quiet and private. Then say, "Sometimes forgiveness is really hard. But once we forgive, we can feel relieved and free. It's better not to worry about the situation anymore; let God worry about it. He wants to! When you truly forgive a person, it feels so good. I betcha can't forgive just one!"

Materials
photocopies of page 27, pencils

Take It to the Next Level

Have students turn to Week 3 in their manuals. Ask the students to write one thing they need to ask forgiveness for. Then have them write the name of one person they need to forgive. Play the mood tape as students complete the page.

When the students have finished, voice a prayer based on Ephesians 4:6, 7. Say, "Lord, thank You for teaching us about anger. Help us to act right even when we are angry. Help us not to sin. Please teach us to take care of our anger quickly, so it will not grow. We don't want Satan to win over us. In Jesus' name, amen."

Materials
"My Mood Manuals," pencils, Bible, mood tape, candle

Video Clips

It's a Mad, Mad, Mad, Mad World. Show any of the humorous "angry" scenes. (Can also be found in many old Three Stooges films.)

The Things We Say

Find and read the following Scriptures in the *International Children's Bible* then match each Scripture to the saying it answers.

A Matthew 6:14, 15 **D** Psalm 7:14, 16
B Proverbs 30:33 **E** Proverbs 15:1
C Proverbs 20:22 **F** Psalm 37:1, 3

1 "I'll get you for this!"

2 "I'll never forgive you!"

3 "Just wait till Mom gets home!"

4 "He gets away with murder. It makes me so mad!"

5 "Oh yeah? Well, you're a jerk!"

6 "I've got a plan to get even with him."

Do any of these phrases sound familiar? Is there someone you need to forgive?

Did you remember to ask God to help you forgive with His own power?

Fear (Courage vs. Crumpling)

Memory Verse. Hebrews 13:6

Know why Jesus said, "Don't be afraid" so many times.
Feel confidence about facing fear.
Replace fear with positive action.

Note to the Leader

A moment of evaluation with your students might be in order. Since emotions tend to snowball (i.e., when one feeling runs wild it tends to lead to another), your students may have been feeling out of control or anxious on several levels. How about checking to see where they are after the first three sessions on this topic? If they have been able to claim some help from any of the first three sessions, they may have found that dealing with one feeling or problem has helped another. Today's session is about fear. Perhaps some of the fears your students had one month ago have diminished in light of the first three sessions. It would be interesting to find that out before actually dealing with the topic of fear directly.

Get Into the Game

Select one of the following activities to introduce today's topic.

Activity #1—Lion Heart or Scaredy Cat?

To play this game, appoint one person to be the Lion Heart. Everyone else is a Scaredy Cat. The cats can run or hide. The Lion Heart tries to tag the cats. When Lion Heart captures a cat, he says, "I give you courage" (pronounced *kkkuh-rudge* as in the classic, *The Wizard of Oz.*). Upon being tagged, each cat becomes a Lion Heart and tries to capture other cats. Continue until all the cats have become Lion Hearts.

Lead into the session by saying, "Fear makes us run and hide. It's kind of fun in a game, but not in real life. Today we're going to see how God can help us with this emotion of fear and turn us all into Lion Hearts."

Materials
access to large, open area

Activity #2—Pet Project!

Prior to the session, contact someone in your church or community who owns an exotic pet such as a snake, spider, or iguana. Ask them to bring their animal to the session. (Note: Be sure this person is knowledgeable about the animal and is comfortable handling the pet around a group of students.)

As your guest displays the animal, ask these questions.

1. How many of you own or would like to own this type of animal? Why or why not?

2. Would everyone in your family be happy if your brought an animal like this home as a pet?

3. Why do you think some people are afraid of these animals? (They don't know much about them; they have a bad reputation.)

After the students have had an opportunity to see (and touch, if appropriate) the animal, say, "As you might have guessed, today's topic is fear. Did you know that most of our fears can be overcome by knowledge? The more we understand about a person, an animal, or a situation (such as flying), the less likely we are to be afraid. Jesus knew we would have fears. That's why we can read His words, 'Do not be afraid,' so many times in the New Testament."

Materials

an exotic pet or animal (e.g., snake, spider, iguana) or TV, VCR, and videotape of a nature program that includes these types of animals

Step 1

Tell the students, "Since we're talking about fear today, we're going to look at a brave Bible hero, Joshua. Joshua became leader after Moses. He led thousands of people. He had to face many scary situations. But listen to what the Lord told Joshua at the very beginning: 'Remember that I commanded you to be strong and brave. So don't be afraid. The Lord your God will be with you everywhere you go' (Joshua 1:9, *ICB).* Apparently Joshua really tried to do what God said. Can you recall some of the great things that happened in the book of Joshua?" (crossing of the Jordan River—Joshua 3:16; fall of Jericho—Joshua 6:20; the sun stood still—Joshua 10:13, 14).

"Any of those situations would have been really scary. Joshua got through them by sticking close to God. I think Joshua's courage influenced the others around him. At the end of the book (Joshua 24:31), we learn that the other people stayed close to God throughout Joshua's lifetime and even long after he died."

Materials

Bibles

Step 2

Distribute photocopies of the maze (page 33). Take turns calling on different students to read the Scriptures aloud. Fill in the blanks as you go.

Materials

photocopies of page 33, Bibles, pencils

When the blanks are filled in, go back and read the phrases in their entirety (e.g., "When I am afraid of the dark, I will remember that the Lord is light").

Then say, "Isn't that great! Does that give you confidence or make you feel any better? It helps me! How can we use what we just learned the next time something scary happens?"

Discuss the possibilities. Some ideas are: read this sheet once a week as part of our daily devotions so it will be on our minds; imagine a panic pause button so that, instead of acting on the fear, we can say "Wait a minute. Is this really something to fear?"

Close by saying, "We forget that the God of the whole universe is right beside us, and we have His power in us. Many adults suffer from fear because they haven't practiced turning over their fears to God. Let's promise to work on coping with fear while we are young. Doesn't that sound like a good idea?"

Step 3

Select one of the following activities to help your students apply what they have learned. Use both options if your have time to do so.

Activity #1—No Big Deal

Tell the students, "We're going to practice a little exercise. You can do this on your own whenever you find yourself getting overly fearful about something. I need a *brave* volunteer to share something he is afraid of or worried about."

Have something in mind, in case no one speaks up. The goal of this exercise is to blow the fear so far out of proportion that it becomes ridiculous.

For example, Sarah is afraid to try out for cheerleading. The student to her left should say something like, "Yeah, cause if you try out, you might fall and everybody will laugh at you." The next student adds, "And then it might come out in the paper that Sarah is the klutziest person who ever tried out for cheerleading." Then the next student says, "And then Sarah would have to move away and live alone in the mountains."

When Sarah's plight has made the rounds *(and hopefully everyone is laughing),* say: "So, Sarah, what about trying out for cheerleading? It's no big deal, right? Do the rest of you really think any of those things are going to happen?" Try another case or two, if students are willing.

Close by saying, "This is a fun way to attack our fears head on and laugh at ourselves. Then, when we can laugh and some of the pressure is off, we can settle down and think straight. We can remember some of the things God has taught us about fear."

Activity #2—Baby Steps

Say to the students, "In the movie *What About Bob?* Bill Murray plays a bizarre guy named Bob. It doesn't take much for Bob to be overwhelmed, to get all bent out of shape. So the psychiatrist teaches Bob the technique of baby steps. For example, if Bob were afraid to go somewhere, he should take the first baby step of standing up. The second step is to open the door, and the third step, leave the house. But, in the movie, the funny part is that when Bob takes his baby steps, he actually takes baby steps, walking in little tiny steps. Let's see if we can use this idea of baby steps to help us with situations we're afraid of."

Discuss ways students could back up from overwhelming, scary situations in order to stop looking at the huge picture and, rather, just begin to deal with it by taking one baby step. (Then, hopefully another. And another. And so on.)

It is best if students will offer their own phobias or upcoming scary situations. Then let the rest of the class suggest the first (or first two or three) baby steps.

You may need to get them started with this example: A person is afraid of snakes, but wants to conquer the fear. The first baby step would be to look at an encyclopedia picture of a snake. Second, do it again tomorrow. Third, touch the picture of the snake.

Another example: A student would like a summer job, but is nervous about the whole idea. The first baby step would be to ask one adult friend to inform him of any summer job openings. Second, circle classified ads that sound interesting. Third, make one phone call about a job.

Close this time by saying, "Fear can completely paralyze us. But the baby-steps idea is a simple way we can overcome our fears. Will you remember to use this the next time you're afraid?"

Materials
video clip from the movie *What About Bob?*, VCR

Take It to the Next Level

Have students turn to Week 4 in their manuals. Ask the students to list a fear they have and Scripture from this session that might help over come that fear. Play the mood tape as the students finish the manual. Encourage students to take their manuals home this week and to refer to them when emotional, angry, or afraid.

When students have finished, light a candle or dim the lights. After a moment of silent meditation, pray a prayer similar to this one, based on Psalm 56:10, 11: "Dear Lord, we praise You for Your Word. Thank You for teaching us. We trust You—so we don't want to be afraid. We know that we will face scary things

Materials
"My Mood Manuals," pencils, mood tape, candle, Bible

and scary people. But what happens to us is not important as long as we stay close to You. Help us to not be afraid. In Jesus' name, amen."

Video Clips

The Wizard of Oz. A scene featuring the lion.

What About Bob? The psychiatrist tells Bob to take baby steps in a situation rather than being overwhelmed by the entire situation.

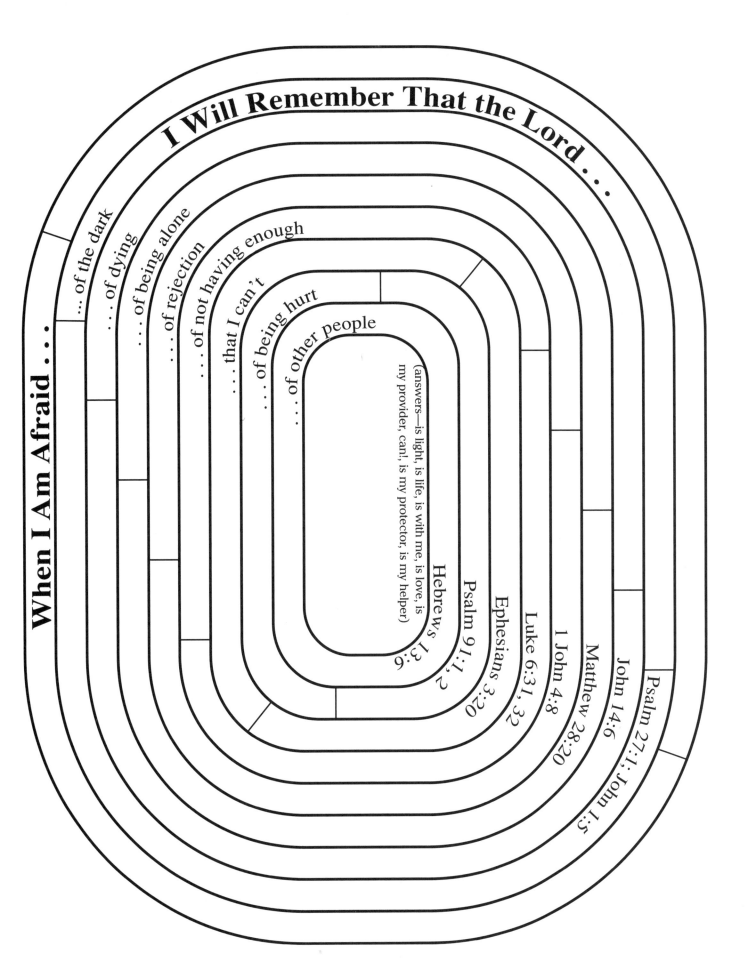

When I Am Afraid . . .

I Will Remember That the Lord . . .

. . . of the dark

. . . of dying

. . . of being alone

. . . of rejection

. . . of not having enough

. . . that I can't

. . . of being hurt

. . . of other people

(answers—is light, is life, is with me, is love, is my provider, can!, is my protector, is my helper)

Hebrews 13:6

Psalm 91:1, 2

Ephesians 3:20

Luke 6:31, 32

1 John 4:8

Matthew 28:20

John 14:6

Psalm 27:1; John 1:5

Bridge the Gap
Family Respect

Scripture. Proverbs 1:1-5, 7a; 16:32; 17:1

Session Purpose

The purpose of this session is to incorporate parent involvement and reinforce what your students have been learning about their emotions. This session can benefit the entire family.

Although the session is designed in the same fashion as the previous sessions, you may want to include an opening time of Scripture reading and praise singing. This may help to unite the group.

Get Into the Game

No matter what your program is for this session, you can begin with this ice breaker.

As you begin your opening comments, tie a knot in the shoestring; then hand it to the first person in the audience, instructing him to tie a knot and pass it on. Reclaim the shoestring when you finish speaking.

Your comments should include: a welcome to the parents, any introductions you feel necessary, a brief summary of the unit topics, and your purpose in having this joint parent-child session. As you move into introducing tonight's program, reclaim the shoestring.

Say, "Would anyone like to try and pick all these knots loose? Me, neither!" Discard the shoestring. "Our emotions can make us feel as if we are all tied up in knots. One little knot isn't so bad. But emotions tend to build until we're so knotted, we don't know where to begin to untie them. We hope tonight's session will be beneficial to your entire family

Materials
long throw-away shoestring

34

and help you to create an emotionally healthy, knot-free atmosphere at home."

Step 1

Enlist senior high students to act as a panel for this session. (Your students will be happy to have young people as "judges"; and the parents will be pleasantly surprised at how fair they try to be.) Be sure and thoroughly explain to the panel your procedure for this session.

Parents and their children need to sit on opposite sides of the room; the panel should be front and center. You are the group leader.

Before class, write on the chalkboard some of your students' least favorite parent responses (e.g., "Be careful," "Turn down that music!" "Don't wait till the last minute").

Open the session by saying, "This class has been studying the topic of emotions. As individuals, we've learned a lot. In this session, we'd like to suggest some improvements for the emotional atmosphere in our homes.

"We're going to let the students air some of their gripes about things they hear at home. We want them to share how hearing these responses makes them feel. You parents will have a chance to explain your reasoning behind your words, as well as your feelings. We also want to know how you feel when your child responds to what you have said.

"Helping us through this session will be our capable panel." Introduce the panel members, if necessary. "The panel will offer suggestions and compromises. Then we want the parents and children to agree on some new strategies at home."

Guide this session, calling on various people in the group, then on panel members. Keep it moving and lighthearted.

The group may want to agree to have a follow-up/evaluation session at a later day.

(Senior highers who are not appearing on the panel could help by serving punch and cookies.)

Materials
chalkboard, four senior high teens to act as the mediating panel

Step 2

This activity encourages your students to work with their parents as a family unit.

Distribute a photocopy of the family pledge (page 38) to each family. Say to the group, "Parents and kids usually have a long list of expectations for each other. When everyone knows what the other expects from them, then they can work together at maintaining harmony. Right now, work together to develop four or five goals your family will attempt to follow to

Materials
photocopies of page 38, pencils

achieve emotional harmony in your home."

Give the families some examples if they have trouble coming up with ideas. For example, The Jones Family set these goals:

1. Hear everyone's side of the story before passing judgment.

2. Set specific house rules that everyone helps to develop and live by.

3. Use "I" statements instead of "you" statements when disagreeing or arguing.

4. Have a devotional/quiet time as a family.

5. Spend at least one night a week together as a family.

When the families have finished, ask for some volunteers to read their ideas. Encourage families to post their commitments in a prominent place at home.

Step 3

Distribute photocopies of page 39 and pencils to the group. Explain that there are many kinds of personality tests. This sheet will use four kinds of runners to illustrate basic personality differences.

Have each person read the descriptions of the four types of runners and place a checkmark by the words that best describe each person. Say, "Although we all have similarities, there are subtle personality differences that make each of us unique. Some of us might make good sprinters, while others would do better running relays. These same differences can create conflict within our families when we don't recognize and accept them."

Ask the group members to look at the words they checked and decide whether or not they are a sprinter, long-distance runner, relay runner, or hurdler. Then make these comparisons:

1. A hurdler son may wonder why his relay runner mom is so uptight. He is rowdy, but she is sensitive and needs some quiet time.

2. A sprinter dad may be a very driven, workaholic-type of man. But his long-distance runner daughter is calmer, slower. They get on each other's nerves, each unable to understand what is wrong with the other.

A serious part of this session should include gratitude for the variety of strength in each family and commitment to work on the weaknesses.

Materials
photocopies of page 39, pencils, chalkboard

Take It to the Next Level

Have your families plan a Power Supper (that's God's power). Families will select one mealtime per week to review and preview each person's schedule. During the supper, each person quickly names high points and low points in his past week. The rest of the family offers congratulations and sympathy/encouragement. A preview of upcoming events should follow. This is a great time to share fears.

Emphasis should be placed on sensitivity. If one member is facing a particularly rough week, suggestions can be made for ways the others can help him through it.

Close your Power Suppers with a short prayer.

Closing

Close this session with a prayer based on Ephesians 3:16-20: "Lord, we know that You are rich with power. We thank You that You happily share Your power with us to strengthen us inside. We know You love us. Help us to remember that, with You, we can do much, much more than we think we can. You are awesome forever and ever. In Jesus' name, amen."

The

Family will attempt to:

1.

2.

3.

4.

5.

Sprinter	**Long-distance runner**
quick	patient
impulsive	good planner
excitable	introvert
aggressive	thoughtful
decisive	controlled

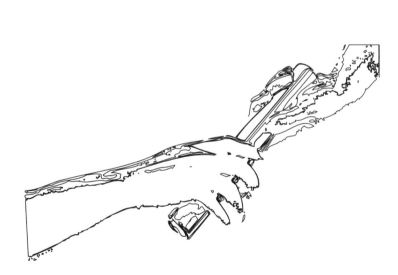

Relay runner	**Hurdler**
team player	risk taker
analytical	outgoing
self-disciplined	enthusiastic
detail-oriented	optimistic
dependable	responsive

Setting the Stage for Service

Note to the Leader:

Use information from this section to talk to your class about service.

A group of junior high and senior high students went to church camp one year. It was a regular camp: they had chapel time, took classes of their choice, went swimming and hiking. They had a great time.

The next year, the same group went to a different kind of camp—a work camp. You couldn't exactly call this camp fun. Some of the students had to clean up a shack where an old man had been living. The cleaning included shoveling rat droppings. Some of the campers prepared skits and music, then visited nursing homes. The campers had to sit and talk with the residents after the performance.

Painting and fixing a run-down church building was part of the project. Still other campers took care of poor street children in a crowded, disorganized day care center.

After this week, sponsors asked the campers which kind of camp they preferred, which they wanted to do again next year. Guess what? They all voted to go to work camp again!

What do you think they got out of work camp that they missed in regular camp? How did work camp affect the way they felt about themselves? the way they felt about others?

We have a bad habit of thinking about ourselves too much. Our emotions take over, and we feel helpless, unimportant, and miserable.

But when we help others, something happens to us. We begin to feel powerful. We have the power to affect someone else's feelings. We have the power to make someone feel loved, accepted, and happy.

Service Projects

The projects suggested all focus on the emotional needs of others. Some of your students may need a reminder to put some of their own feelings aside (e.g., shyness, embarrassment, inadequacy, fear). Encourage students to concentrate on others instead of themselves as they serve.

Card Project

Choose a group related to your church for whom your class is going to purchase cards. (This could be the missionaries your church supports, the sick, or all the members of a certain Sunday school class.) During a class period discuss this group of people and the kinds of sentiments that need to be conveyed to them.

Then go on a card-buying trip. Encourage the students to choose cards appropriate to this group's feelings.

Arrange for the cards to be addressed properly and mailed.

Meter Magic

When a person comes to his parked car, discovers his meter has expired, and has gotten a ticket, he may feel angry, sad, or frustrated. For this outing, the class goal is to spare the people in your town these negative feelings.

Supply students with coins. Have them walk your downtown area for a predetermined period of time. After they've combed a specific area, have them meet back together thirty minutes later.

Go for burgers or ice cream. As you eat, discuss the meter experience. Were any of the students caught in the act? What happened?

If time permits, you can return and re-do the same meters or go to another location.

Celebrating Senior Saints

Your class is going to have a party with the senior citizens group from your church.

Your class can serve the seniors a light meal in the fellowship hall, enlist another class to serve the entire group, or use a meeting room at a local restaurant.

If your class is eating with the seniors, be sure the seating arrangement mingles the two groups. Use assigned seats, if necessary.

After eating, each senior will share a personal account of his most embarrassing moment, saddest moment, or the scariest thing that ever happened to him.

This can be a contest. After all the "most embarrassing moments," for example, students will vote on the best one. Prizes can be awarded in each category.

Student interviewers can also ask questions: "How long did you feel embarrassed about what happened?" "How did you get over being sad?" "After being so scared, what did you do to stop feeling spooked in similar situations?"

It is hoped that, through this activity, the seniors will enjoy sharing some of their wisdom—and have a good time! For the students, it may be enlightening to see that "old people" have feelings, too. At a later time, ask for student input about the event. What did they get out of it? How do they think the seniors felt about it? Can the class think of other ways to help the senior citizens as a group or individually?

It's the Little Things

This requires a planning and discussion session.

Decide on some acts of service that your students could perform for your church.

Discussion should include how these acts would contribute to the emotional growth of the students, as well as what emotional benefit the congregation would receive. Here are some possibilities.

1. Greeter. One of your shy students may want to direct visiting kids to their proper Sunday school classes. (Remind your students that if they are shy in the familiarity of their own church, how much more uncomfortable a new student might feel.) Of course, a new student who is met by a friendly face gains confidence and feels as if someone cares.

2. Big Brothers and Sisters. Students would be assigned to families in your church who have small children. On Sunday mornings, they would assist the families in hanging up coats, carrying diaper bags, or helping little ones to their classes.

3. Please Come Again. Let your class take over the task of writing visitor follow-up cards for a quarter. Work together to create messages that convey real feelings (e.g., "Wasn't Sunday a great day!" or "We think the music at our church is cool. We're glad you were here to enjoy it with us").

Operation: New Kid at School

Your class will develop strategies for welcoming any new kids at their schools. If your students are from different schools, that's even better! They can pair up by schools. Their goal is to put themselves in the place of the new student, to try and understand all the feelings he must be experiencing.

Then, with your help, class members can practice welcoming a new student, offering to help show him around, and inviting him to church.

You may want to make this an ongoing project, with students reporting throughout the school year.

Unit 2

Scripture. 1 Corinthians 13:4-7;
Ecclesiastes 4:9, 10; John 15:13-15;
Proverbs 17:17; Romans 5:8;
Philippians 2:3

Know the world's rules and God's guidelines for being a friend.
Feel convicted to become a godly friend.
Work on being the kind of friend God
says is good.

Kids today may have more trouble than previous generations
applying God's Word to their lives. They have access to more
information. They have grown up in a society of instant gratifi-
cation. They live in a world where there are no examples or
standards for God-based values and morals. They are expect-
ed to automatically know the best choices when they have little life experience and often lack confidence to decide. God's
Word addresses most of these issues with well-defined value
statements. These four sessions identify Bible people who
made both good and bad choices. One session is a study of
helpful adjectives that characterize people who practice making good choices. The other three sessions focus on individuals who decided. When we imagine what their thinking
process might have been, some helpful patterns emerge for
us. The supplemental family session and service project sections are filled with ideas that will make the concepts taught
in the first four sessions very practical. Try to accomplish at
least one service project during the time your class is studying
this unit. Or better yet, take a service project idea and imple-
ment it into each session. The sessions will become fun and
very practical.

Session Plans

Each of the four sessions is prepared to help the teacher introduce the Bible passage and quickly involve students in an
activity. The Scripture study follows. The application is the most
important section for helping students' make good choices. In
every session the word and letters **S.T.O.P.** are used. It intro-
duces an easy-to-remember catch phrase to encourage students to **S**top, **T**hink and pray, **O**ptions (examine your options),
and **P**ick the best choice.

Each of these principles is discussed and applied in a style that assists students to make careful choices rather than spur-of-the-minute choices. We want the students to leave each session knowing that they can make the best possible choices when they can think and evaluate the consequences.

Devotional Suggestions

The thirty-one days of devotional suggestions (pages 46–48) will help students build a strong foundation, identifying characteristics of God's love for them. Because God's love is so great, we respond by loving Him back. When we love God, it is easier to make good choices.

Photocopy one set of the three reproducible pages for each student. Encourage each student to try to complete the devotional suggestions each day.

Daily Devotions

Day 3

God loves you so much that He knows all of your needs. Read Matthew 6:25-34.

Day 7

Read John 3:14, 15. I know that God loves me because He has prepared an eternal home for me.

Day 4

We must choose to love and serve only one God. Read Matthew 6:24. Is there another god in your life?

Day 8

We show God that we love Him by obeying His commands. Read John 14:21.

Day 1

Read John 3:16. Instead of reading, "For God so loved *the world . . . ,*" insert your name and read, "For God so loved *Debbie.*" Insert a family member or friend's name.

Day 5

God and Jesus are one body but separate. That means that both of them love you, *really* love you. They work together so that everyone, everywhere might believe that Jesus is the Christ, the Savior of us all. Read John 17:20-23.

Day 9

Read John 15:13. The greatest example of love is expressed in this verse. What is it? Who has done this for you?

Day 2

Because God really does love me, I can love Him back. Read Matthew 6:22-37.

Day 10

Read John 15:10. I can show Father God and His Son, Jesus, my love by obeying Their commands.

Day 6

Because Jesus is God's Son and my Savior, I love Him more than my family, friends, and things. He is my first love. Read Matthew 10:37-39.

Day 14
What does God ask of you? Read Deuteronomy 10:12, 13 to find out. Instead of reading, "And now, *O Israel*," read, "And now, *Debbie*."

Day 17
Exodus 20:3 is the first of Ten Commandments that are to be our responses to God's love for us. What do we do?

Day 20
The world does not honor this Commandment. Many things are available to keep us from worshiping God together on the Lord's Day. Exodus 20:8 says to remember the Sabbath. Christians are to remember the Lord's Day, Sunday. Is there something that hinders your from keeping God's Commandment?

Day 13
The rich man, who loved his possessions was still loved by Jesus our Savior. Jesus loves us even if we don't love Him as we should. Read Mark 10:21.

Day 16
Read John 15:12. If we love God, then what do we do?

Day 19
The subject of Exodus 20:7 happens every day all around us. Do you have a problem with mis-using God's name? If so, what do you need to do?

Day 12
Luke 16:13 says that we cannot serve two masters. Read Luke 16:13 and think about the Master who really loves you.

Day 11
Read John 10:11-15. Are you following the Good Shepherd or are you following the hired hand?

Day 15
Read John 14:15. If we love God, then what do we do?

Day 18
Exodus 20:4 is another of the Ten Commandments that God established. What is the problem? Do you have anything that is more important to you than God?

Day 21

Exodus 20:12 is an easy way to show God how much you love Him. Read it and begin honoring your parents. How do you honor your parents?

Day 25

What is another way to say, "Do not give false testimony against your neighbor" (Deuteronomy 20:16)? Exodus 20:16 includes honesty in private and public issues.

Day 28

Colossians 3:12-14 lists several ways to show God's love to other people. Do you see some ideas for things you need to work on?

Day 22

Read Exodus 20:13. This Commandment deals with more than the physical side of killing. Jesus said that being angry with someone is murder because we assassinate their character (Matthew 5:22). Use words cautiously.

Day 29

Read John 5:19-23. Jesus lived as God wanted and honored His Father. Christians, who identify themselves with Jesus, must honor and live as Jesus would have us live, making right choices.

Day 26

To covet is to wish to have the possessions of another so much that you are resentful if someone has certain possessions and you don't. Exodus 20:17 says that such attitudes are against God's law.

Day 23

Read Exodus 20:14. On television and in the movies this often happens. Acts of sexual impurity break God's law and destroy people's lives. Keep this Commandment for life.

Day 30

James 1:5 tells us " . . . if anyone lacks wisdom, . . ." we need to ask God and He will give us wisdom generously and ungrudgingly. Most adults would tell you that they seek wisdom from God, especially when making decisions.

Day 27

The Holy Spirit produces the character traits mentioned in Galatians 5:22, 23. These characteristics are the result of our love for Jesus and His workings in us. Which qualities do you desire?

Day 24

Exodus 20:15 means that we ought not to take things that do not belong to us, but it goes further than physical things. Think about things like stealing time or stealing positive, uplifting words from people. Think about other things that may be stolen to hurt someone.

Day 31

Would you be one who is doing your best so that God names you as one of His approved decision makers? 2 Timothy 2:15 says that we need to be doing our best.

The Race of a Million Choices

Scripture. Jonah 1, 3; Galatians 5:16-18; 2 Timothy 2:15

Identify the bad choices and, later, the positive decisions made by Jonah.
Feel empowered to make godly choices.
Design a plan for making godly choices.

Get Into the Game

Before class, gather several items that students might identify with (tennis ball, camera, cassette or CD player, measuring cups, sheet music, videotape, book, markers, sports equipment, shoes or shoelaces, thread and needle, hammer and nails, a fishing pole).

Display these items on a table in an area away from the students. Make a sign to display over the area titled, "Choices."

Ask students to gather in a circle.

Distribute an index card and pencil to each student. Ask them to examine the display of items and choose one item that tells something about themselves. As students return to the circle, ask them to write their names on the index cards. One at a time, dismiss the students to place their name cards by the item they chose. Be sure they have turned their name card upside down. The purpose of this game is to match the student to the object he chose.

If a student's first choice is taken, ask him to make a second choice. After each class member has placed his or her name card by an object, ask the class to go to the table and guess who might identify with each object. Have each student tell something about himself and why he chose that particular item.

When everyone has finished say, "You just chose something to be identified with, something the rest of the class will remember about you. We choose clothing, hairstyles, shoes, and words that identify us each day. We choose to obey or disobey. We choose to listen or not to listen. We choose to let God be part of our lives or not to let Him in.

"We serve and follow God because He is perfect. We serve and follow God because of who He is. He is holy. He is pure. He is just. He is complete. He is God. He loves us just because He is God.

Materials
items that characterize each student (see list), index cards and pencils, a sign labeled "Choices"

"We respond to Him by following His example. We respond to Him by obeying His teachings. We respond to Him by trying to do everything as we know He would want. He loves us and we love Him.

"Adults and kids who love God and want to serve Him experience the constant struggle that Paul writes about in Galatians 5:16-18. Those who love God and live by the leading of the Holy Spirit struggle each day between serving God and serving selfish desires. The battle happens when sinful desires get in the way. Things get out of control when decisions are made without thinking about the consequences, examining the possibilities, and praying for help.

"For example, everyone loves to eat sugar and the wonderful sweet treats made from processed sugars. But many of us have experienced the trauma of sitting in the dentist's chair. We have experienced the roar of the drill as the dentist fills a cavity in a tooth, all because we chose to eat sugar. If I had thought about the consequences of eating all that candy before popping it into my mouth, I might have saved myself many hours in the dentist's chair. When I take time to think about each decision and pray for God's leading and wisdom, I usually make much wiser choices than when I simply react."

Step 1

God wanted to use Jonah as His messenger. Read Jonah 1:1, 2 and put the boat in the water to float with the words, "Jonah is sent by God."

Jonah chose not to obey God's directions and developed his own plan to avoid God. Read Jonah 1:3 and place the boat in the water to float with the words, "Jonah runs away."

God used drastic measures to get Jonah's attention. The sailors were so afraid of dying that they forced Jonah to tell what he had done that displeased God. Read Jonah 1:4, 8-12 and place the boat in the water to float. Write the words, "Storm threatens everyone," on the plate.

The superstitious sailors did everything possible to keep from throwing Jonah overboard, but were not successful. They finally took the necessary action to calm the storm. They threw Jonah out of the boat. Read Jonah 1:15-17 and place the boat in the water to float with the words, "Jonah is punished."

After three days and nights in the belly of the fish, God had the fish throw up an unharmed Jonah. God had cared for Jonah by keeping him safe and placing him on dry land. Read Jonah 2:10 and place the boat in the water to float with the words, "Jonah is delivered."

"What had Jonah learned? What do you think Jonah prayed

Materials
five Styrofoam meat containers or plates to be used as boats, a wading pool or tub of water, Bible

after the ordeal? Jonah learned a tough lesson. His decision to disobey God almost resulted in a shipwreck and loss of several sailors' lives. He almost lost his own life, all because he chose not to obey God. Jonah had made a wrong choice.

"The good news is that Jonah's story has a happy ending. He was given a second chance." Read Jonah 3:1-3. "Jonah went to Nineveh and preached repentance to the people, who listened and stopped doing wrong."

Step 2

"God does not speak to us in an actual voice, telling us what to do. He spoke to Jonah in an audible voice because the Old Testament people did not have the written Word of God. New Testament people did have Jesus Christ in the flesh. Today, God speaks and has spoken to us through His written Word, the Bible. We have the Word as a testimony of Jesus' teachings.

"When we make a decision, God does not intervene to change our minds. He can use all of our experiences for good (Romans 8:28), and He does not zap us with punishments or bad experiences so that we will make choices that are best.

"Jonah chose not to listen to God. God caused specific physical problems for Jonah that helped Jonah change his mind and decide to obey God's directions. If we choose to disobey God and participate in any activity that we know is wrong, the natural consequences of a bad choice may result in a bad event or experience."

Divide the group into smaller working groups. Using magazine pictures, create a collage of pictures that represent the good and bad choices kids make. Some suggestions include music or reading materials, smoking, drinking, movies, videos, television shows, types of friends, places to hangout.

In the small groups, discuss the consequences of bad choices. For example, smoking has been medically linked to many kinds of diseases and is considered an unhealthy choice. Telling lies results in a personal character that cannot be trusted. We want to be known as trustworthy people who are true and honest.

Materials
magazines, glue, poster board

Step 3

Keep the same small working groups and distribute a sheet of red poster board to each group. Instruct the group to draw a stop sign. Letter the sign with the word *stop* spelled out vertically. Mount the completed stop signs on the walls of the room. Ask for a volunteer to write the words on the sign as you direct the following discussion (see example in margin on page 52).

Materials
red poster board, markers, photocopies on red paper of page 53, video camera, blank tape

Tell the students, "When we are about to make a decision, there are a few good rules to remember. The first is to **Stop**! Someone may ask you to do something or go somewhere. Before answering, practice this by stopping.

"**Think and pray!** Ask God for help. Then ask yourself, 'Does this choice honor God? Am I making the best choice? Am I being truthful? Am I being obedient? Does the action show self-control? Am I demonstrating boldness?'

"**Options!** Examine your options. If you answer positively to the questions, then it is probably a great choice. If you answer negatively to one question, then you need to think of another option.

"**Pick!** When all answers to the questions are positive, go for it! When one answer is no, pick another activity, look for another choice, choose to leave or turn it off."

Distribute photocopies of "S.T.O.P. Signs." Ask students to complete the words or phrases for **S.T.O.P.** that will help them remember to stop when making choices.

As students complete their pages, discuss what might have been different with Jonah and his story if he had practiced the **S.T.O.P.** technique. What questions would Jonah have asked? What might Jonah have prayed? What other options might Jonah have explored? What would have been Jonah's first choice?

Take It to the Next Level

Use the following situations to practice **S.T.O.P.** with the students. They may work in a role play setting or general discussion. Do not limit your class to these suggestions. Encourage students to do their own creative role plays and practice the **S.T.O.P.** If available, videotape the role plays and use them for discussion in future sessions.

Role play suggestions:
1. Friends are shoplifting.
2. The guys at the sleep-over are making obscene phone calls.
3. The girls at the sleep-over are reading dirty magazines.
4. No one is home so you can watch restricted television.
5. Friends are trying cigarettes.
6. You find some pills and "joints" in a plastic bag.

Second Timothy 2:15 tells us to be "workmen who are not ashamed, who handle the Word of truth correctly." Instead of workmen, change the phrase to "fifth and sixth graders, who are not embarrassed to be bold Christians."

Gather your group together in a huddle and pray for each student that they will be able to use the **S.T.O.P.** this week to make great choices.

Materials
camcorder and video tape (optional)

Signs

Session 2

The Pressure Is On

Scripture. Daniel 3:1-30; Galatians 5:16-18

Identify the choices made by Shadrach, Meshach, and Abednego and the challenges they encountered because of their choices.
Feel empowered to make the same kind of good choices as Shadrach, Meshach, and Abednego.
Make a commitment to live for God even when the price is high.

Get Into the Game

Distribute photocopies of "What's Hot, What's Not!" Begin discussing things that were peer pressure issues when you were in fifth or sixth grade. For example, I remember that to leave the house with Mom's approval, the skirt was an inch above the knees. Once at school, we would race to the rest room and roll the skirt up at the waistband so it would be the acceptable mini-skirt length.

(Sharing a personal example may help students realize that you experienced the very same things they do today.)

Ask the students, "Why do we do things to be just like everyone else? What is it that causes us to do and act in ways that we know are not best? How can trying to be exactly like everyone else harm us?

"We serve and follow God because He is perfect. We serve and follow God because of who He is. He is holy. He is pure. He is just. He is complete. He is God. He loves us just because He is God.

"We respond to Him by following His example. We respond to Him by obeying His teachings. We respond to Him by trying to do everything as we know He would want. He loves us and we love Him.

"Adults and kids who love God and want to serve Him experience this constant struggle that Paul writes about in Galatians 5:16-18. We who love God and live by the leading of the Holy Spirit struggle each day between serving God and serving selfish desires. The battle happens when our sinful self gets in the way.

"It is all right to want to be accepted and popular, until other people become more important than God. In Daniel 3:1-30, King Nebuchadnezzar asked the people to make him more important than God. Shadrach, Meshach, and Abednego shared a conviction that bound their allegiance to God, and

Materials
photocopies of page 58, pencils

they chose to die rather than deny their God. They made a choice to live for God, no matter what happened to them."

Step 1

Materials
photocopies of page 59

Ask for student volunteers to act out the parts of the astrologers, herald, King Nebuchadnezzar, Shadrach, Meshach, Abednego, and the narrator. Nonreader parts are needed for the strong guards and the angel.

Distribute photocopies of the script (page 59) to those who volunteered to act. Read the script together, acting it out, and then discuss. Ask the following questions:

1. What laws of God were the people being required to break? (Exodus 20:3).

2. Why did the king want the people to worship him?

3. Why is it against God's law to worship someone or something other than the true God?

4. What could Shadrach, Meshach, and Abednego have said or done in order to save their lives? *(We will bow down but not actually worship the idol; We will only do this one time, but we won't become idol worshipers, then ask God for forgiveness; The king has absolute power and we must obey him. God will understand; we're not hurting anybody!)*

Tell the students, "Shadrach, Meshach, and Abednego chose to take the most costly position. They chose to risk their lives, disobey King Nebuchadnezzar's order, and follow God's law exactly as He intended.

"Choices such as bowing down but not actually worshiping the idol, bowing down just this once, or trying to make excuses for a poor choice may seem like the best decisions. What damage would bowing down to the idol do? Who would have known if Shadrach, Meshach, and Abednego would have bowed to the idol? Let's think about it. God knows when we make poor choices, and many times other people around us see and know when we make poor choices. The non-Christians often watch Christians hoping to see them 'mess up' just to ease their own conscience. By making poor choices, Christians send a message to nonChristians that we do not want them to see. What message might Christians send to fellow Christians if they chose to disobey God's law?"

Step 2

Materials
poster board and markers or chalkboard and chalk, paper, pencils

"When we face situations that challenge our Christianity and witness to others, many other people are affected by our choices.

"By choosing to be faithful to God and His teachings, Shadrach, Meshach, and Abednego made an impact on many people. They chose to live for God. They chose to die for God."

Ask students to help you make a list of the decisions and the results of those decisions made by Shadrach, Meshach, and Abednego. On a poster board or chalkboard, write this phrase, "The decision not to worship King Nebuchadnezzar meant that Shadrach, Meshach, and Abednego experienced . . ." Complete the phrase. *(They were rejected, treated like animals, and condemned to death.)* As students suggest ways to complete the sentence, record each suggestion and affirm each student. Then write these open-ended statements on the poster board or chalkboard. "Other believers in God saw . . ." *(three men who were willing to die for God).* Record all suggestions.

Record this open-ended statement on the poster board or chalkboard. Be sure to include all of your student's suggestions.

"Those who did not believe in God saw . . ." *(three men who were willing to die for something they believed in).* And then record this final open-ended statement. "Nebuchadnezzar and the law makers had to . . ." *(re-evaluate their beliefs about God).*

Say to the students, "It is not easy to make tough decisions that go against the crowd. It is not always easy to choose to be different. It is not easy to be the one who enforces and makes the rules. The best solution is to do things God's way. It may not be easy, but the best choices are ones that assist you to live for God."

Step 3

Say to the students, "Last session we learned the **S.T.O.P.** acrostic: **S**top, **T**hink and pray, examine your **O**ptions, and then **P**ick the best choice. When we stop, think, pray, and carefully decide what is best in God's eyes, then we will make good choices."

Ask students to form groups of four. Distribute pencil and paper to each group. Read each of the following situations and ask the group to draw suggestions for making good choices.

1. The most popular kids at school use a certain notebook. You want them to like you. Will you try to talk your parents into getting the exact notebook for you? What would be another way to handle the pressure? (Discuss each group's ideas and drawings. Praise the students' creativity and ask for practical ways to respond to this kind of situation.)

2. Your science teacher says that it is a well-proven fact that man evolved from apes. You don't agree. Will you state your feelings in front of the class? What would be God's way of responding to the science teacher? (Review each group's ideas

Materials
paper, pencils

and drawings. Encourage further discussion about the best solution to this challenge of our Christian faith.)

3. A teacher known for telling corny jokes tells your class a joke that is actually funny. It makes you want to laugh. However, the students have an unwritten rule among themselves. They never laugh at his jokes. Will you break the unwritten rule? What would be the best way to respond to the pressure? (Ask students to explain and review their drawings and solutions to this situation. Discuss appropriate respect for others.)

4. You are invited to a sleep-over birthday party. You want to go. You find out that the hosts will be showing videos that your family would not want you to see. What do you do? What would be the best way to handle this situation? (Examine each group's drawings and ideas for handling this situation. Encourage creative ideas. This is something every preteen has faced or will face.)

With students in small groups, ask them to write a "cheer" about making good choices. After a few minutes, ask each group to perform their "cheer."

Take It to the Next Level

At the conclusion of the session, gather your entire group together in a huddle and pray for each student individually. Ask God to help them be God's kid this week.

What's Hot!
What's Not!

What's really hot at your school? What's most popular with all the kids? What things would most kids in your school never want to get caught doing? Tell something that is "in" and "out" from each category. Which things are very important to you?

		What's Hot!	What's Not!	Important
1	Brand of jacket			
2	Type or name of shoes			
3	Brand name of jeans			
4	Jewelry (guys)			
5	Jewelry (girls)			
6	Hairstyle (guys)			
7	Hairstyle (girls)			
8	Musical group			
9	Way to spend money			
10	Activities with friends			

Daniel 3:1-30 Comes Alive!

Narrator: All the people of Babylon were assembled for a dedication.

Herald: This is what you are commanded to do, O peoples, nations and men of every language, as soon as you hear the sound of the horn, flute, zither, lyre, harp, pipes and all kinds of music, you must fall down and worship the image of God that King Nebuchadnezzar has set up. Whoever does not fall down and worship will immediately be thrown into a blazing furnace.

Narrator: As soon as the people heard the instruments, they fell down and worshiped the image of God.

Astrologers (to King Nebuchadnezzar): O King, live forever! You have issued the decree but there are some Jews— Shadrach, Meshach, and Abednego— who do not worship the image of gold.

(Enter the strong guards, bringing Shadrach, Meshach, and Abednego.)

Narrator: Nebuchadnezzar was furious and sent for Shadrach, Meshach, and Abednego. They were brought before the king.

King Nebuchadnezzar: Is it true that you do not serve my gods or worship the image of gold? If you do not bow and worship these, you will be thrown into the blazing furnace.

Shadrach, Meshach, and Abednego: O King, we do not need to defend ourselves in this matter.

Meshach: If we are thrown into the blazing furnace, our God is able to rescue us from your punishment.

Abednego: And even if God does not rescue us, we want you to know that we will not serve your gods or worship the image of gold.

Narrator: Nebuchadnezzar was so furious with Shadrach, Meshach, and Abednego that he ordered the furnace heated seven times hotter than usual. *(The strong guards enter and tie Shadrach, Meshach, and Abednego. The strong guards throw them into the fire, and they drop dead from the heat.)* He had them tied and thrown into the furnace. The furnace was so hot that flames of fire killed the men who took Shadrach, Meshach, and Abednego to the furnace. When King Nebuchadnezzar went to the furnace to check things, he was amazed at what he saw and summoned his advisors.

(The angel enters the furnace area with Shadrach, Meshach, and Abednego.)

King Nebuchadnezzar: Wasn't it three men who were tied and thrown into the fire?

Astrologers: Yes, O King.

King Nebuchadnezzar: I see four men walking in the fire, unbound, unharmed and the fourth looks like the son of the gods. *(King Nebuchadnezzar calls towards the furnace.)* Shadrach, Meshach, and Abednego, servants of the Most High God, come out!

Narrator: They came out, and King Nebuchadnezzar's advisors gathered close. They saw that the fire had not harmed their bodies or robes, their hair was not singed, and they did not smell like smoke.

King Nebuchadnezzar: Praise be to the God of Shadrach, Meshach, and Abednego who has sent His angel and rescued His servants. They trusted Him and were willing to sacrifice their lives to worship their own God. Anyone who says anything against the God of Shadrach, Meshach, and Abednego shall be cut into pieces, and their houses be turned into rubble.

Think About These Things

Scripture. Philippians 4:8, 9; Galatians 5:16-18

Recognize words from Scripture that describe people who make good choices.
Feel confident to make good choices.
Practice the plan for making good choices.

Getting Into the Game

Begin by reminding students, "We serve and follow God because He is perfect. We serve and follow God because of who He is. He is holy. He is pure. He is just. He is complete. He is God. He loves us just because He is God.

"We respond to Him by following His example. We respond to Him by obeying His teachings. We respond to Him by trying to do everything as we know He would want. He loves us, and we love Him.

"Adults and kids who love God and want to serve Him experience the constant struggle that Paul writes about in Galatians 5:16-18. We who love God and live by the leading of the Holy Spirit struggle each day between serving God and serving selfish desires. The battle happens when our sinful selves get in the way.

"Statistics say that most adults in Alcoholics Anonymous began their battle with liquor with the innocent sip of a drink at a very young age—about your age. A careless choice made without thinking or the acceptance of a dare from a friend at a party may result in a life of suffering for someone who could not tolerate such things."

Ask students to complete the "Media Maze Survey" (page 66). Tell them that today's session will help them make godly choices in relationship to the things they watch, listen to, and read.

Before class, prepare eight pennant shapes from poster-size paper. Letter each poster with one word from Philippians 4:8, 9. Ask students to find Philippians 4:8, 9 in their Bibles and listen to the words used in the Scripture. These words are all positive, uplifting, encouraging words that tell Christians what to think about.

Materials
photocopies of page 66, pencils

Step 1

Divide the class into six groups. Give each group markers or colored pencils and a pennant. Ask the group to work together to create simple definitions for each word and record them on the pennant.

When the groups have completed the work, pretend with your students that you are the magic genie. You can grant any of the qualities listed on these pennants. Which quality would each of your students want? Why? Listen to each student's response. Record each student's reason for wanting a particular characteristic and why. Discuss these qualities further with the students.

Tell the students, "These words are adjectives. They describe people. They are not action words or words that give us ideas of things to do. Instead these are words that describe what we want to be. To be true, noble, right, pure, lovely, admirable, excellent, and praiseworthy people, there are some very important action steps we must take. When we control our television watching or control the movies and music videos that we watch, we are making choices that help us think about positive things. When we guard the type of books and magazines that we read, we are protecting our minds from filth and danger."

Refer to the survey from the introductory activity. Listen as students tell about the rules their families follow to guard media influences on each other. Reinforce each student's positive contribution and encourage others who do not have quite as many guidelines to begin controlling the time they spend watching television.

Tell the students, "The old saying, 'Garbage in—Garbage out,' applies to us. If we read trashy books and magazines or watch violent and sexually obscene movies, those horrible things rub off on us. If we listen to bad language and dirty stories, we may find ourselves saying things that are not appropriate. What we put into our heads usually comes back in our speech, actions, and attitudes."

Step 2

"In previous sessions, we discussed the **S.T.O.P.** acrostic. It may help us to **S.T.O.P.** before we act. Many mistakes are made when kids react to a situation without first thinking and asking for God's direction.

"**S** is for stop. Stop before making a decision, stop before acting, stop before speaking.

"**T** is for think and pray. Pray and ask God for help. Then

true

noble

right

pure

lovely

admirable

excellent

praiseworthy

Materials
markers, colored pencils, pennants prepared prior to session, dictionaries, poster-size paper cut into eight pennant shapes each labeled with one of the following words: true, noble, right, pure, lovely, admirable, excellent, praiseworthy

think, does this activity honor God? Am I making the best possible choice? Am I being truthful? Am I being obedient? Does the action show self-control? Am I demonstrating boldness?

"**O** is for examine your options. If you answer yes to the previous questions, then it is probably a good choice. If you answer no to one question, then you need to think of another option.

"**P** is for pick. When all the answers to the questions are yes, go for it! When one question is answered with a no, make another choice. Make the best decision possible.

Read these role play situations and discuss how to help these kids demonstrate the qualities from Philippians 4:8, 9. Review the S.T.O.P. process. Suggest ways to assist the students so that they might become the best they can at making good choices.

1. The gals on Jenny's swim team all use God's name in vain. It is too easy to slip and use God's name incorrectly. What can Jenny do? Which quality from Philippians 4:8, 9 could assist Jenny? How could the S.T.O.P. help her?

2. Justin's best friend Dominick listens to music filled with violence, sexual innuendoes, and foul language. Dom is having problems with his behavior and language. What can Justin do? Which quality from Philippians 4:8, 9 can Justin talk with Dom about? How could Justin talk with Dominick about the S.T.O.P?

3. Thad, Nate, and Zack found pornographic magazines in the garage they were cleaning for a neighbor. They all decided to take a break and check out the magazines. Now Nate is having problems with impure thoughts. What can he do? What quality from Philippians 4:8, 9 could assist Nate? How could the S.T.O.P. assist him? What would you suggest that Nate do?

Students may have some personal situations they would like to discuss. Conclude the role play discussion by talking about the choices we make. "God has given us the privilege of free choice. When we make poor choices, He does not zap us or punish us, and He does not intervene to change our minds for us. He does use all of our experiences for good (Romans 8:28). When we allow Him, He can even use wrong choices to help us learn valuable lessons.

"It is not easy to stay true, noble, pure, lovely, admirable, excellent, and worthy of praise. These words from Philippians become very meaningful when we have been tempted and are successful in making the best possible choice.

"Words like 'cool' and 'popular' do not appear in this list from the Bible. Often choosing to be true, noble, right, pure, lovely, admirable, excellent, and worthy of praise will mean that we give up a friendship, a hobby, or an activity that causes us to have serious problems or make wrong choices.

When we stop, think and pray, examine our options, and pick the best activity, we move toward Christ-likeness. Because each of us is in a construction process, there will be times of huge success and times of faltering."

Step 3

During the week, save all kinds of food refuse such as vegetable peels and fruit peels. Put these things into something that seals airtight. Bring two food processors to class. Tell this story or a similar example as you do the following demonstration.

Say, "Faith had two best friends. Aspen and Tara had lived next door to Faith since kindergarten. The three of them walked to school together, talked for hours on the phone, and had slumber parties together. They were inseparable. Faith even brought the girls to church, and they became Christians. It was great!" *(Begin dropping the garbage into the food processor.)*

"Things started to change in the seventh grade. Aspen and Tara started hanging out with other kids. They started smoking, swearing, misusing God's name, and buying questionable magazines. Faith knew these were things her family did not approve of, but it was more important to be with her friends and be one of the group than to do what she knew was right. Her Christian witness was being polluted with garbage."
(When the garbage is all blended, ask for a volunteer to drink it. Hopefully, no one will accept the challenge.)

Set the garbage-filled food processor to the side. Put the other food processor on the table and start putting frozen strawberries, frozen orange juice, five or six ice cubes, a banana, and two tablespoons of sugar into the container. Continue the story. "Faith had a personal relationship with Jesus and realized that Aspen and Tara did not demonstrate the desirable characteristics of a true, noble, lovely, admirable, excellent, or praiseworthy follower of Christ. Faith decided that she had to quit hanging out with Aspen and Tara.

"When we choose to be kids who serve and follow Jesus, we join a team that dares to act differently from the rest of the world. Little helps like the stop, think and pray, examine your options, and pick the best choice may one day keep you from serious trouble."

(Pour small amounts of the strawberry drink into cups for each student.)

Materials
two food processors, food refuse (vegetable peels, fruit peels), frozen strawberries, frozen orange juice, banana, ice cubes, two tablespoons of sugar, cups

Take It to the Next Level

Gather for a time of prayer. Prior to the session, designate eight areas as stations for a prayer walk. Classes that meet during the night could use candles indoors as stations. Classes that meet during the daytime may require some creative planning to set the tone for silence and solitude. Use a closet-type place or set up under a tree in a remote location of the property.

Write the following devotional thoughts on a paper and place them at the appropriate location for each station.

Materials
paper, Bibles, candles and holders, mirror, a gold medal or an award, smoke detector or fire extinguisher, trash can, rocks, VCR and TV, Christian music video

True

Read Psalm 15:1-5. If "living close to God" means being and doing all these things mentioned in Psalm 15, is there anything keeping you from being true to God? *(This station is located in the church chapel or sanctuary.)*

Noble

Read Psalm 32:6, 7. God is all around me. He will help keep me noble if I let Him. *(This station is located in a closet or small place.)*

Right

Read Romans 10:17-19. Pray that you will do what is right and honorable in God's eyes. This will keep you from becoming contaminated. *(This station is located near a smoke detector or fire extinguisher.)*

Pure

Read Psalm 119:9-11. What do you need to do to keep your life pure? *(This station is located in a dark narrow hallway.)*

Lovely

Romans 14:17, 18 says that serving God is one way to please Him and show how lovely or handsome you are. *(This station is located in a quiet place with a mirror.)*

Admirable

The word in Philippians 4:8, 9 is admirable. Do others say that you have a good reputation and that your conduct and attitude are commendable? Could you receive an award for being admired? *(This station is located in a quiet place with a gold medal or some similar award.)*

Excellent

James 1:21 says that we are to get rid of everything that is morally filthy and evil. Replace it with all kind acts. Are there some things you need to throw away? *(This station is located in a quiet place with a trash can.)*

Praiseworthy

Psalm 18:1-3 says that God is our rock-solid source of celebration, applause, and rejoicing. *(This station is located in a quiet place with a pile of rocks.)*

Send the students off one or two at a time with their Bibles. Give directions so that they proceed to each station in order, quietly so as not to disturb each other.

Rent or borrow a Christian music video to play while students wait for their turn to participate in the prayer walk. As students complete the prayer walk, they may enjoy watching the video while waiting for their friends to finish.

MEDIA MAZE SURVEY

1 **How much TV do you watch?**

___ Less than most kids my age.

___ More than most kids my age.

___ About the same as most kids my age.

On weekends?

___ Less than most kids.

___ More than most kids.

___ About the same as most kids.

2 **How many videos do you watch?**

___ Less than most kids my age.

___ More than most kids my age.

___ About the same as most kids my age.

On weekends?

___ Less than most kids.

___ More than most kids.

___ About the same as most kids.

3 **How many hours do you spend listening to music?**

___ I never shut off the music.

___ I have periods of quiet.

___ I hate music.

4 **What rules do you have in your family about TV?**
(Check all that apply.)

___ No TV allowed.

___ I must ask before watching.

___ When the homework is finished—anything goes.

___ Only a few hours each day.

___ No rules at all.

___ Other _____

5 **Fill in the blank with the word *often, sometimes* or *never*.**

I _____ watch television shows that are not good for me.

I _____ listen to music that is not good for me.

I _____ read books and magazines that are not good for me.

Choices That Serve God

Scripture. Luke 10:25-37; Galatians 5:16-18

Know that people who profess to love and serve God don't always make good choices.
Feel empowered to make good choices.
Choose to be a kid who makes good choices.

Get Into the Game

Before class, put a sign on one wall that says, "Maybe." On another wall, place a sign that says, "Maybe not." Ask students to walk to a wall where the sign is displayed that states how they would respond to each of these statements.

1. All kids nine years and older should be allowed to stay up as late as they want on any day of the week.

2. Kids can spend their allowance any way that they want.

3. Kids are allowed to go to school only when they want.

4. Kids are allowed to eat any kind of food at any meal they want.

5. Kids can have as many bikes as they want.

6. Kids get to watch all kinds of movies.

Record how many students said maybe and how many said maybe not for each statement. Bring the group back to their chairs to discuss each statement.

Review each statement and the number of students who decided maybe and maybe not. Ask the students, "How did you come to your decision? What were some questions or things you thought about as you decided maybe or maybe not?" Discuss the pros and cons of each statement.

"Parents have rules and guidelines at home, teachers have rules, our country has laws, and even the motion picture industry has ratings. All of these are to protect us and keep us safe. Every day we decide whether or not to obey the rules and guidelines.

"We serve and follow God because He is perfect. We serve and follow God because of who He is. He is holy. He is pure. He is just. He is complete. He is God. He loves us just because He is God.

"We respond to Him by following His example. We respond to Him by obeying His teachings. We respond to Him by trying to do everything as we know He would want. He loves us, and we love Him.

Materials

signs with the words "Maybe" and "Maybe not"

"Adults and kids who love God and want to serve Him experience the constant struggle that Paul writes about in Galatians 5:16-18. We who love God and live by the leading of the Holy Spirit struggle each day between serving God and serving selfish desires. The battle happens when our sinful selves get in the way.

"Many times decisions are made without thinking. For example, after the game the gang hangs out at the fast food restaurant next to the school. The coolest kids are there, and so are the cigarettes and 'joints.' The pressure to smoke is incredible! You know that smoking is associated with all kinds of diseases and is against the law for underage children. But the pressure is still overwhelming.

"Today, we want to discuss ways to be good thinkers and prayers when challenging times of decision-making occur. Better decisions are made when we have thought about our response. Poor decisions are usually made when we act on the spur-of-the-moment."

Step 1

Collect eight paper plates. Number the back of each paper plate one through eight. Then write the corresponding instructions on each plate:

1. Read Luke 10:25-29 aloud for the class.

2. Tell what happened in the Scripture just read. What question was Jesus asked? Why did the man ask, "Who is my neighbor?"

3. Read Luke 10:30 and summarize Jesus' story so far.

4. Read Luke 10:31 and summarize.

5. Read Luke 10:32 and summarize.

6. Read Luke 10:33-35 and summarize what happened in Jesus' story.

7. Read Luke 10:36 and answer Jesus' question.

8. Read Luke 10:37. What word did the lawyer use to describe the Samaritan? What did Jesus tell the lawyer to do?

Fly each paper plate like a Frisbee disk in correct order to discuss and read the Scripture study. Ask the class to participate in the Scripture study by following the directions and replying to the statements or questions.

Capsulize the events of Jesus' story. "Jesus used this story to illustrate the kind of attitude He wanted all people to demonstrate toward each other. We are studying this story to determine how each person made choices and responded to a person in need."

Materials
eight numbered paper plates with instructions written on them

Step 2

Begin the application time by thinking about the choices the priest, Levite, and Samaritan faced. Each one encountered the same situation. Each one made a specific choice. Use the **S.T.O.P.** principles of Sessions 1, 2, and 3 to determine the best choices.

Distribute the photocopies of "Samaritan S.T.O.P." Ask students to look at the first outlined figure and label it: Priest. Priests served in the temple by offering the sacrifices for sin. Look at the **S.T.O.P.** outline and have students answer these questions.

1. Did the priest stop? (*We are unclear, so question marks are appropriate.*)

2. Did the priest think? Did he pray? (*We are unclear, but he may have thought about the problems associated with getting involved with this man.*)

3. What were some ways he could have handled this situation? What could the priest have done? Do you think he attempted to examine his options?

4. What did the priest choose? (*He did not get involved.*)

Next have students to look at the second outlined figure and label it: Levite. Levites were so named because they were from the tribe of Levi. They assisted with the maintenance of the temple services and order. Ask students the same questions and record the information.

1. Did the Levite stop? (*Once again, we are unclear, so a question mark is appropriate.*)

2. What did the Levite think? Did he pray?

3. What were the Levite's options?

4. What did the Levite pick?

Now have students look at the final outlined figure and label it: Samaritan. Samaritans were Jews who lived in the land of Samaria. They had intermarried with Gentiles, so they were not pure Jews. Because they were not pure Jews, they were hated by Jews.

Again, ask the questions.

1. Did the Samaritan stop? (*Yes.*)

2. What did the Samaritan think? Did he pray? (*We are unclear, but he must have thought about caring for the injured man.*)

3. What were the Samaritan's options? (*He could have left the injured man to die or take him for help.*)

4. What did the Samaritan choose to do? (*He chose to attend to the man's injuries and help him.*)

Now ask the students these summary questions.

1. Which man made the best choice? (*The Samaritan.*)

2. How did you determine that the Samaritan's choice was best? (*He took time to plan a way to help even when it required time and money.*)

3. What did it cost the Samaritan when he chose to get involved? (*Time, money, effort.*)

4. Why was this the best choice of all three situations? (*He showed kindness to a fellow human being. He was a helpful neighbor to someone in need.*)

5. Which command from God did the Samaritan exhibit? (*Deuteronomy 6:5; 10:12, 13; Leviticus 19:18.*)

6. In Luke 10:37, the lawyer who asked Jesus the questions that began this session used a word to describe the Samaritan. What is that word? (*Mercy.*)

7. When we make a choice that uplifts God and shows our Christ-like character, it usually costs something. What did it cost the Samaritan when he chose to show mercy for the injured man? (*Time, money, and friends because Samaritans did not usually show kindness to the Jews.*)

Refer to the example of the ball game used earlier in the session. Say, "After the game, all the gang hangs out at the fast food restaurant next to the school. The coolest kids are there, but so are the cigarettes and 'joints.' The pressure to smoke is incredible! What process could you use when deciding what to do? What questions and options are available to you? What are the best choices you could make?"

Tell the students, "Someday you may have to make a choice that will cost time, money, or even friends. Deciding to make good choices is not always the easiest answer or the easiest way out. Being a Christian may not always be the most popular or the easiest decision. It may cost you friends, time, extra effort, and even money. We can make good choices when we take time to stop, think and pray, examine our options and pick the best choice."

Step 3

Gather the group together in a semicircle for a time of encouragement. Honor each student by encouraging and uplifting him for one magnificent minute. Designate one student to be the honoree. Direct that student to a special chair at the head of the semicircle. As the student sits, remind the class that this is one minute to tell encouraging things you have noticed about this person. Tell something good or something you appreciate about this person. The purpose of this activity is to encourage students so that they will make good choices this week. Be sure that each student has an opportunity to sit in the encouragement seat for one magnificent minute.

Materials
one chair in the center or at the front of the room

Take It to the Next Level

Before class, prepare instant pudding, enough for each student. Provide a variety of ingredients so that the class has many items to choose for toppings (e.g., nuts, shredded coconut, whipped topping, chocolate chips, peanut butter chips, butterscotch chips, or marshmallows). Instruct students to make choices to create their own delicious treat.

As students eat and enjoy, review the S.T.O.P. method. Ask about tests at school or special activities that are planned for this week that might be especially challenging. Be sure to ask questions and make suggestions that will assist students to make good choices. Close in prayer, praying specifically for each student's upcoming challenges.

Materials
instant pudding ingredients and toppings

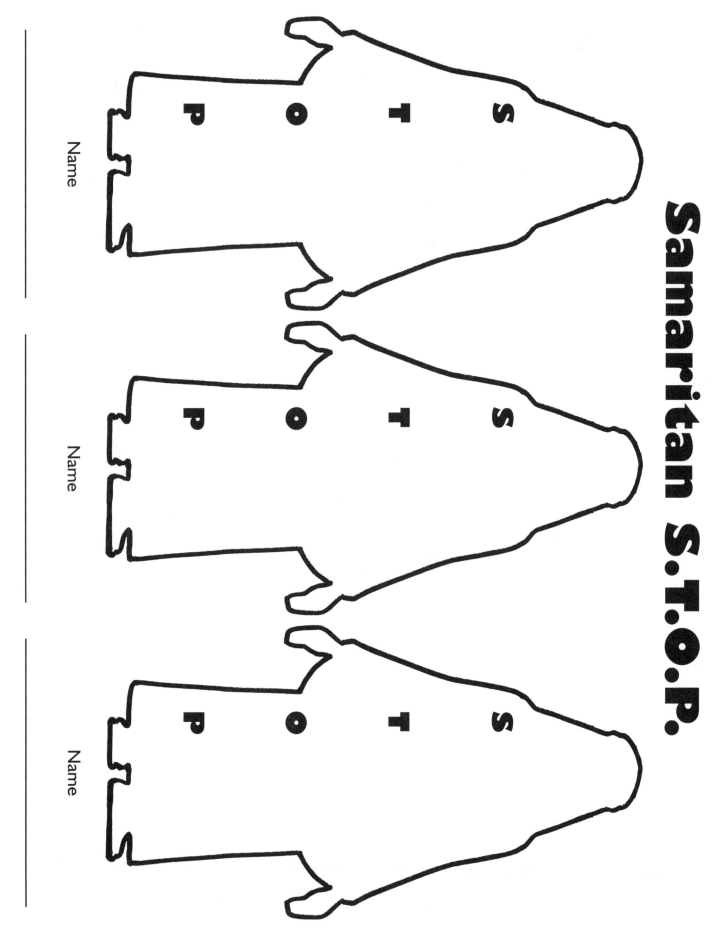

Samaritan S.T.O.P.

Family Choices

Choose from the following suggestions and activities to practice making good choices.

Devotional Ideas and Discussion

Read Hebrews 13:18, then pray each section of this verse for each student. Pray that Joe has a clear conscience, Samuel chooses to act honorably in all things, etc.

Discuss what a clear conscience means by asking the following questions.

1. What does your conscience do? (*gives you a sense of right and wrong*)

2. How do you describe a clear conscience? (*free from guilt and worry*)

3. How do you describe a hurting conscience? (*nagging feeling of guilt*)

4. How does one who acts honorably behave? (*with honesty and integrity*)

5. What is honorable behavior? (*a good reputation; showing a sense of right and wrong*)

6. Hebrews 13:18 is a prayer that Christians are honorable in all things? What are the boundaries on the words "all things"? (*there are none*)

7. Name some "all things" activities where we are to act honorably? (*speech, schoolwork, recreation time, etc.*)

Choices Meal

Plan a meal where many choices are offered. Enlist the entire families' help to plan and prepare a smorgasbord-type meal. Some suggestions include: pasta with several different choices of sauce, a lettuce salad or baked potato with several different toppings, and several types of bread with various flavors of butter, jelly, and jam.

A party atmosphere would be fun. Provide a variety of dishes, table service, drinks, and glasses or cups. Encourage the group to be adventurous, making all kinds of choices.

At the close of the activities, review the number of choices each person made. The reward for having made the most choices is the leftovers. The person who made the most choices gets to take the leftovers home.

Choices Journal

Keep track of all the different choices made in one day. Declare one day of the week, "Choices Day." Provide small notebooks for each participant. Every time a choice is made, write what was chosen in the notebook.

At the end of the day or the next class session, review the choices each person made. Younger children may prefer keeping track of their choices by making a refrigerator chart. Every positive choice earns a sticker.

Recount any choices that were made using the **S.T.O.P.** method. Determine which were spur-of-the-minute choices. Label each decision as good, better, best, or not so good.

Choices Maze

Convert a room at church or a room in a garage or house into a maze using ideas similar to a spook house or mouse trap game. Make a maze using tables and boundaries with choices that lead to a dead end or the way out. Use doors and tunnels or corners to create the maze.

Make the maze more difficult by having students crawl on their hands and knees. Blindfold students or have them go through the maze in a wheelchair or on crutches.

Mats or old mattresses will make a challenging maze. Refrigerator boxes or boxes from a furniture store may also assist students as they build a choices maze. Invite friends and neighbors to experience the choices maze. At the end of the adventure, discuss how to make good choices.

Television Decision

Distribute photocopies of "Television Decision." Locate the television guide from the local newspaper for the next few days. Read descriptions of two or three select shows or two hours of programming on MTV. Ask students to write the name of one of the television shows that they think they may like to view under the heading, Television Program. Use the **S.T.O.P.**

method to evaluate whether this program is valuable or "not so great" for their viewing. "**S** represents stop. It is easy to stop here, but it is not always so easily done when channel surfing. Choose the facial expression from the border of the page that best describes how you feel and draw it in the 'stop' box. **T** represents think and pray. Ask these questions: Why do I want to watch this? Will I be a better person after watching this? Choose the facial expression from the border of the page that best describes how you feel and draw it in the 'think and pray' box. **O** represents options. Examine your options. Based on the answer to these questions, I choose to watch the program or do something else. What other things could I be doing? Choose the facial expression from the border of the page that best describes how you feel and draw it in the 'options' box. **P** represents pick. What do I pick to do? Choose the facial expression from the border of the page that best describes how you feel and draw it in the 'pick' box. What do you choose to do, watch television or do something else?"

The "What if . . ." Game

Role play these examples of situations and then discuss the choices and options available in each situation.

1. Marguerite agreed to meet Hannah after school, but instead Marguerite decided to go to the soccer game with Angela without telling Hannah. *How did Marguerite's decision affect Hannah? How does Hannah probably feel toward Marguerite? What would have been a better option for Marguerite?*

2. Jameel decides to cut in front of Ashantee in the cafeteria line. *How does Jameel's decision affect Ashantee? How is Ashantee's attitude toward Jameel affected? What would have been a better choice for Jameel to have made?*

3. Your best friend, Candace, decides to steal a candy bar from the store while you are shopping together. *How does Candace's decision affect you? How do you feel about Candace? What would have been the best thing for you to do?*

4. Samantha and her sisters decide at the same time that they both want the last piece of brownie. *What needs to happen so that there is not a fight? What is the best thing to do?*

There are almost always several choices for us to make. They may not always be the choice of our dreams, or our favorite choice. Learning to look for more possibilities will help us lead happier lives. Some choices are significant and some are simple. Some choices are crystal clear. Some are black and white. It is very important to learn to look for options. Read Colossians 3:1-4 and pray together.

Television Decision

Strong Decision

Confusion

Frustration

Indecision

Anger

Joy

Television Program	S	T	O	P

Go to Extremes

Choose to Serve

Select any of the following activities to use with your students.

Choice Bucks Shopping

Photocopy and cut the "Choice Bucks" (page 79). Make one copy so that each student will have $75.00. Students will use the "Choice Bucks" to shop at the Character store.

Save empty vitamin and pill bottles, empty food cartons and boxes. Label each empty container with the following characteristics: loving heart ($50); patience ($25); able to make good choices ($50); honest ($25); morally pure ($25); a truth teller ($25); kind ($25); considerate ($25); gentle ($25); peaceful ($25); self-controlled ($25); boldness ($25); forgiving ($25); cheerful ($25); generous ($25); a hard worker ($25); strong ($25); obedient ($25); faithful ($50); and wise ($50).

Make as many containers of each characteristic as you wish. Price each item accordingly.

Give each student $75 in "Choice Bucks." This amount represents $1 for each year that they may live. Ask students to decide which quality from the items displayed they would most like to possess. When students go shopping, they may not spend more than the $75. Make selections, pay the shopkeeper, and take purchases back to their seats.

As students pay using their "Choice Bucks," pray aloud for that person. Ask God to give the students the qualities they have chosen and purchased.

When everyone has paid, ask the following questions?

1. Why are the qualities you chose important to you?
2. How can these qualities help you make good choices?
3. How do you get these qualities in real life?

Good Choice/Bad Choice

Plan a field trip to the local video store. Divide the group into teams, one adult to each team. Ask each team to find two videos and evaluate them using the **S.T.O.P.** method. You could also include a trip to a music store, a newsstand, or a bookstore.

Review the **S.T.O.P.** steps. "**S** stands for stop. It is easy to stop when the group is evaluating the video, but not always so easy when looking at so many choices, especially if friends are there. It is always best to have a good idea and a plan when entering the video store. Plan which video you want to rent. If it is not available, have another choice ready as a back-up.

"**T** stands for think and pray. Ask these questions: Why do I want to see this video? Can Jesus watch this with me? Will I be a better person after watching this video?" Pray and ask for God's help.

"**O** stands for examine your options. Is there another video that would be better to see?

"**P** stands for pick. Rent your best choice. Take the videos back to someone's home. Watch and enjoy."

Survey

Distribute photocopies of the "Choice Survey" (page 80). Use these sheets to conduct a survey of several adults or peers. Ask for help with a project your class is doing. Ask them to answer these questions, then record their responses on the sheets. The questions are:

1. When you have to make a tough decision, what do you do?
2. Whom do you talk with when you have to make tough decisions?
3. What are some things you think about or questions you ask when making a tough decision?

Have students survey their peers, adults in the church, grandparents, teachers at school, older friends, and acquaintances.

After the students have conducted the survey, have them come together to discuss the results. Ask for things they learned from each question. Record students' summaries on the board or a large sheet of paper. After hearing from each student, ask them to examine the list and select one or two ideas from each of the three questions. Distribute a **S.T.O.P.** sign and have the students record tips learned from this survey on the back or bottom of their reproducible sheets.

Choice Bucks

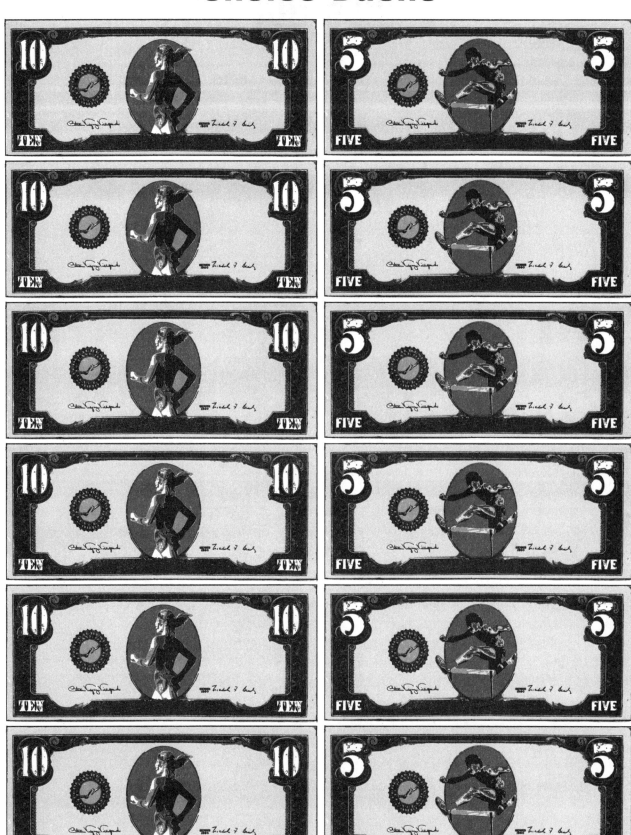

Choice Survey

Name _____

1. When you have to make a **tough decision,** what do you do?

2. Whom do you talk with when you have to make **tough decision**s?

3. What are some things you think about or questions you ask when making a **tough decision**?

Unit 3

Truth Relay

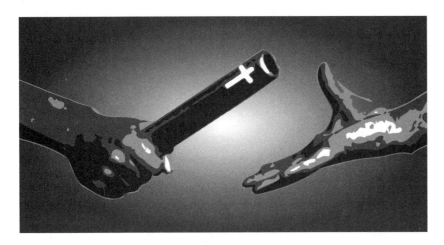

"Always be prepared to give an answer to everyone who asks you . . . ," asserts Peter (1 Peter 3:15, 16). These four sessions will prepare your students to give an answer when faced with issues that challenge their faith. Nearly every student will have to deal with the four prominent issues discussed in these sessions—evolution, care of the environment, ways to God, and the history of the United States of America. Each session was developed in response to information your students face concerning these issues—in school, on television, from friends, and in the books and magazines they read.

Each session is designed to give your students a strong base of knowledge concerning the issue—both biblical knowledge and knowledge gained from science or other research. Knowing about the issue will strengthen their belief and will give them confidence to speak out about the issue.

In addition, through learning the unit verse, 1 Peter 3:15, 16, the students will discover a Bible formula to help them stand up for their faith. Memorizing and discussing this verse are integral to the success of each session.

However, the sessions are intended to move beyond knowledge. Your students will be encouraged to stand up for their faith by practicing role play situations.

Although you can't guarantee what your students will do outside the classroom, the knowledge and skills you give them during these sessions will greatly increase their confidence in real-life situations.

How the Sessions Work

This unit is slightly different from the first two. These sessions include experiments, role plays, and games. The following short descriptions will help you become familiar with the parts of the sessions.

Get Into the Game

The booth provides a unique way to introduce each session. Before the students enter the door of the room, they must fill out a ticket relating to the session. Tickets are on reproducible page 95 and complete instructions are in each session.

Step 1

Through activities such as science experiments, games, or drama, students discover scientific or other research related to the topic.

Step 2

Students learn what the Bible says about the topic and relate it to the information they discovered in Step 1.

Step 3

Through games and other activities, students memorize and understand 1 Peter 3:15, 16. They'll discover the formula for standing up for their faith.

Step 4

Students work in small groups to role-play situations based on each session's topic.

Take It to the Next Level

Students create or gather something they can take home to encourage them to stand up for their faith.

Additional Activity

A fun, active game is suggested that relates to the session. The optional game can be used anytime throughout the session.

Book Fair

Call your local Christian bookstore and ask if they would be willing to participate in a Book Fair. Provide copies of the resources listed on pages 7 and 8, as well as other resources your bookstore offers. An ideal time to plan the fair would be before and after the Bonus Family Session. Make a sheet to send home with your students listing the resources that will be available and giving a short description of each one. Parents and students can examine the sheet ahead of time and come prepared to buy the resources that interest them.

Guest Teachers

For an enriching and valuable addition to this unit, invite a Christian teacher or teachers from your church or community to visit your session. If possible, have a different teacher visit each session. Tell the teachers the topic of the session ahead of time and ask them to come prepared to share (1) how they stand up for their faith in the classroom, and (2) ways students could respectfully stand up for their faith. The teacher could share after Step 3 in each session.

Bookmarks

The next two pages contain four reproducible bookmarks that suggest personal study time for your students. Give the appropriate bookmark to your students at the end of each session. Encourage them to think of a specific time each day when they can use their bookmarks to help them read their Bible and pray to God.

Week One

Sunday
Read Genesis 1:1-13. Use all the words you can think of to describe a plant God made. Thank God for the plant.

Monday
Read Genesis 1:14-25. Use all the words you can think of to describe a bird or fish God made. Thank God for the bird or fish.

Tuesday
Read Genesis 1:26-31. Use all the words you can think of to describe a person you know that God made. Thank God for the person.

Wednesday
Read Job 38:22-30. Write your own description of the weather God made.

Thursday
Read Job 39:19-24. Choose an animal you like. Write a description of the way God made your animal.

Friday
Read Matthew 10:29-31. What does God know about your hair? Thank God for 5 other things He knows about you, His creation.

Saturday
Read Romans 1:19, 20. What wonderful things do you see in creation that help you know about God?

Notes

Week Two

Sunday
Name 5 things you see every day. Read Psalm 24:1. Whose are they?

Monday
Read Psalm 24:1 and try to say it from memory. Name 5 people you know. To whom do they belong?

Tuesday
Read Psalm 24:1, then say it from memory. Name 5 famous people. To whom do they belong?

Wednesday
Read Genesis 3:19. What was God's recycling plan for man? Name 3 other items that eventually become dust.

Thursday
Read Isaiah 55:10. What part of God's world needs water to live? How is the water that isn't used eventually recycled?

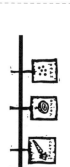

Friday
Read Genesis 1:26-30. What are 2 things you can do to care for God's earth?

Saturday
Read Psalm 24:1 and say it from memory. Thank God for 3 things He created in the world.

Notes

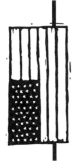

Week Four

Sunday
Name some kings you have heard of or studied. Read Psalm 47:7-9. Who is King of all the earth?

Monday
Read all the printing on a penny, a nickel, a dime, a quarter, a dollar. Now read Psalm 56:11. What are some things a nation could trust in? Who does our nation trust in?

Tuesday
Read Psalm 33:12-19. What good things happen to a nation that trusts in God?

Wednesday
Read Proverbs 14:34. What makes a nation great? What makes a nation a disgrace? Is our country great, or is it a disgrace?

Thursday
Write 3 things you can do to help our nation trust in God. Read Proverbs 3:5.

Friday
Name some times it is hard to stand up for your faith. Read Proverbs 3:5 and try to say it from memory. Who understands even when we don't?

Saturday
Name some times you must decide to do right. Read Proverbs 3:5 and say it from memory. Where does your help to do right come from?

Notes

Week Three

Sunday
Read Acts 4:10, 12. What is so special about the name of Jesus? Thank God for this wonderful name.

Monday
Read John 14:6. Thank God that He gave you a way to get to know Him.

Tuesday
Read Romans 3:23. Have you sinned? Who else has sinned? Who takes away our sin?

Wednesday
Read Titus 3:5. Name some good things you have done. Do they make you good in God's eyes? What makes you good in His eyes?

Thursday
Read Romans 1:20. What can every person in the world see that helps him or her to know about God?

Friday
Read Luke 14:15-24. What excuses have people used to avoid spending time with God? What does God do about people with excuses?

Saturday
Read Acts 4:12. Read it again. Now try to say it from memory. What is the name the verse is talking about?

Notes

Standing Up for Creation

Memory Verse. 1 Peter 3:15, 16

Know that scientific evidence supports the fact that the world was created by God.
Feel confidence in responding to faith challenges.
Role-play answers to those who believe the world evolved.

Before You Begin

Check the recommended resources for this session on pages 7 and 8. It will be extremely helpful to have the materials pertaining to this session available for reference.

If at all possible, look at the science textbooks your students are using so that you can prepare specific answers to the questions they will be facing at school.

You may also want to tailor the role plays to meet their needs.

Get Into the Game

Before the session, make a sign on the poster board that says, "Ticket Booth" in large letters. In smaller letters write, "You must fill out a ticket to be admitted."

Photocopy and cut out the tickets from page 95, one for each student. Save the tickets for Sessions 2–4 to use in those sessions.

Snap the models apart. Assemble one model and leave the other model in pieces. Place both models on the ticket booth table.

As students arrive, have them take a ticket, write the answers to the questions, and put the tickets in the box.

Students do not need to write their names on the tickets.

Materials

two identical snap model kits (dinosaurs would be appropriate for this session), poster board and markers, photocopies of the ticket for this session from page 95, a shoe box or other cardboard box with a hole for the tickets cut in the lid, pens or pencils

Step 1

Set up the following lab experiments in different areas of your room. Instructions may be printed on a card for Experiment #1, and students can complete it on their own.

At least one adult will need to be present at Experiments #2 and #3.

Experiment #1—Just the Right Size

Follow these instructions:

1. Work in groups of three to do this experiment.

2. Choose a black circle and a yellow circle. The black circle is the moon. The yellow circle is the sun.

3. Place a masking tape strip on the floor. This is the earth. Measure 12 inches and place another masking tape strip on the floor. This strip is the moon. Then measure 36 inches beyond the second strip and place a third masking tape strip on the floor. The third strip is the sun.

4. One person should stand on the first strip. A second person should hold the moon and stand on the second strip. A third person should hold the sun and stand on the third strip.

5. The first person should have persons 2 and 3 hold the moon and sun up so that they are at his eye level. Then the person with the moon should slowly move it until it is directly in front of the sun. What do you see? Trade places and let each person observe the moon and sun. Write what you see.

6. Now move the sun 12 inches closer to the moon and move the moon in front of it. What do you see? Move the sun 12 inches farther away from the moon. What do you see?

Conclusion: The sun is about 400 times bigger than the moon. The sun is about 400 times farther from earth than the moon. This means that the moon is exactly big enough to cover the sun during an eclipse. We don't know why God chose to make the sun and moon this way, but they are an example of the perfect order of the universe.

Materials

two black construction paper circles, eight yellow construction paper circles, measuring tape, masking tape

Experiment #2—
Why Cats Don't Bump in the Night

Follow these instructions:

1. Look in the mirror at your eyes. Notice the dark part in the center of your eyes—your pupils. How big are they?

2. Now look at the bright flashlight for a minute. Look in the mirror again. How big are your pupils now?

3. Cover your closed eyes with your hands. Count to sixty. Now look in the mirror. How big are your pupils?

4. Look at the cat's pupils in the photo. How big are they? How do they look different from your pupils? Write why you think they are shaped differently.

(optional)

5. Bring the cat near the light. (Have an adult supervise this part of the experiment.) How big are his pupils?

6. Take the cat to a darker place (the hall or a room without windows). How big are his pupils?

7. Why do you think our pupils get bigger in the dark and smaller in the light? Whose pupils changed size more quickly—

Materials

flashlight, mirror, photo of a cat's eyes (optional: arrange for a friendly cat to visit your class)

yours or the cat's? Who do you think would see better in the dark?

Conclusion: God designed our pupils to allow just enough light in so we can see our best. When it is dark, our pupils get bigger to let in more light so we can see better. When it is light, our pupils get smaller to keep too much light from getting in our eyes. A cat's pupils change much more quickly and get much larger and smaller than ours, partly because of the way they are shaped. God made the cat's eyes this way so that he can see to hunt in the dark.

*Experiment #3—*The Right Spin

Follow these instructions:

1. Stand on the outer part of the Sit 'n Spin. Hold your arms out straight from your sides. Have someone slowly spin you around in a circle. Once you are spinning, quickly pull your arms down straight to your sides.

2. What happened when you moved your arms? Why do you think you came off the Sit 'n Spin?

Conclusion: Your hands were like the earth orbiting around the sun. Your body was like the sun. The earth is spinning exactly the right speed and is exactly the right distance from the sun to keep it moving around, or orbiting, the sun. If the earth were closer to the sun, it would be flung into the sun, just like you were flung off the Sit 'n Spin when you moved your arms closer to your body. If the earth were farther away from the sun, it would go too slow and fall away into space. God placed the earth exactly the right distance from the sun.

Materials

Sit 'n Spin toy (If you do not have access to one, they are available at most toy stores for $10-$20, and would make a great gift for a preschool relative or friend after this session.)

Step 2

Gather students in a large group. Open up the ticket box and read several of the answers on the tickets. Ask students, "Was the question on the ticket hard to answer? Why or why not?" *(No, because it was very obvious which model you worked on.)*

Hold up the dinosaur model that you completed. Say, "In one way, this model is like the world that God created. When we look at the world, it is very obvious who made it and put it together." Ask students to find Romans 1:20 in their Bibles. Read the verse aloud together, then ask the following questions:

1. How does this verse say we can understand God? *(by what He has made; the world that He created)*

2. What can we understand about God? *(His power; His nature)*

3. It's so easy to learn about God through His creation that we don't have any of what? *(excuses)*

Materials

globe, lamp

Now read verse 23 together and answer these questions:

1. What did the people in the Bible decide made the earth instead of God? (*images or idols in the shape of men or animals*)

2. What do some people today believe made the earth instead of God? (*Explain that many people believe the earth began by a big explosion, so that everything on earth came into being by chance.*)

3. Hold up pieces of the dinosaur model that you did not assemble. Ask, "If a big wind blew through our classroom, do you think the wind could blow these pieces together in the right way to assemble the dinosaur?" (Let students speculate. Explain that, according to mathematical calculations, there is actually a much greater chance that a wind could assemble the dinosaur than the world could have been created from nothing. In fact, some mathematicians have calculated the chance that life could come into being all by itself is 1 with 130 zeros after it to 1.)

Ask students to turn to Genesis 1 in their Bibles. Use the globe as you discover facts about the earth.

Read Genesis 1:1-8, then discuss these questions:

1. What was the expanse that God made? *(the sky, our atmosphere)*

2. Explain that there are two important gases that make up the atmosphere that begin with the letter O. One we breathe, and the other is a layer that protects us from the sun. Ask students to guess the two gases. *(oxygen and ozone)* We can breathe oxygen, but it doesn't protect us from the sun, so God put oxygen right where it needed to be—down close to the earth. Ozone is poisonous for us to breathe, but it protects us from the sun. God put ozone right where it needed to be—up above the oxygen on the earth. No other planet has oxygen or ozone!

Read Genesis 1:9, 10. Explain that no other planet has liquid water. Point to the globe. Ask students to guess what would happen if the earth were completely flat. *(It would be totally covered with water.)*

Read Genesis 1:11-19 and choose student volunteers to demonstrate what they discovered about the position of the earth, moon, and sun in experiments #1 and #3. Explain that there are other reasons why God placed the earth exactly the right distance from the sun. Turn on the lamp and place the globe near it. Tell the students, "This lamp will represent the sun for our earth. What do you think would happen to the weather on earth if it were closer to the sun?" *(It would be much hotter. In fact, if the earth were closer to the sun, the whole earth would be a desert. There would be no water, no plants, and no life.)*

Did You Know?
In 1981, 86 percent of people in the United States wanted creation to be taught in our schools. Only 8 percent of people wanted only evolution to be taught.

Move the globe much farther from the lamp. Ask the students, "What do you think would happen to the weather on earth if it were farther from the sun?" *(It would be much colder. If the earth were farther from the sun, everything would freeze. No plants could grow, and no animals or people could live on earth.)*

Ask students to look at verse 14 again. Say, "What do you think God meant when He said the lights in the sky would be for signs, seasons, days, and years?" *(Let students respond.)*

Explain that the way the earth moves around the sun determines time for us. Spin the globe around and explain that it takes one day for the earth to spin around one time. Then move the globe around the lamp while it is spinning. Explain that it takes exactly one year for the earth to move all the way around the sun.

Where the earth is around the sun also determines what season it is. Hold the globe on one side of the sun. Tip the northern hemisphere away from the sun. Say, "Which part of the globe gets more light? What season do you think it is on that part of the globe? Which part of the globe is darker? Which season is it on the darker part of the globe?" *(It is summer on the southern hemisphere and winter on the northern hemisphere.)* Demonstrate how the seasons are switched when you tip the northern hemisphere of the globe toward the sun.

Read Genesis 1:20-31 and choose student volunteers to demonstrate what they discovered in experiment #2 about how God made our eyes and the special way He made cats' eyes.

(Note: If your students need more activity during Step 2, set up a live model of the earth, sun, and planets instead of using the globe as described. Demonstrate how the earth revolves around the sun each year, rotates on its axis every day, and how the tilt of the axis causes the seasons. Students can work in pairs. One student will be the sun. Provide small flashlights for the suns. The other student will be the earth. The earth will spin around. Explain that this takes one day. Then the earth will begin orbiting around the sun, while he is still spinning around in circles. Explain that it takes one year for the earth to move all the way around the sun. If the "earth" can lean to the right while spinning and orbiting, the seasons can be demonstrated as well.)

Step 3

Print the memory verse phrases on the three colors of poster board strips as follows.

Red—In your hearts/set apart Christ as Lord.

Materials
photocopies of the bottom of page 95, three different colors of poster board strips (red, blue, yellow), scissors, tape, a marker

Blue—Always be prepared to give an answer/to everyone who asks you/to give the reason for the hope that you have.

Yellow—But do this with gentleness and respect,/keeping a clear conscience,/ so that those who speak maliciously/against your good behavior in Christ/may be ashamed of their slander.

Before the session, cut the bottom half of reproducible page 95 into four strips. During the opening experiments, give four outgoing students one of the strips and ask them to speak in order (1-4) later in the session. Encourage them to try and memorize what they say rather than read it from the paper. Choose a signal to let student #1 know when to speak, such as looking at him or raising your hand.

Before this activity, tape the ends of the red poster board strips to the ceiling, so that they are hanging from the ceiling. Tape the blue strips to the floor. Tape the yellow strips at various places around the walls of your room.

As students gather in a group for this activity, give the signal for student #1 to say his line from the reproducible page. The three other students you have chosen should jump in and respond to the student.

When the students have completed their drama, thank them and let the class know that they were acting according to your directions. Ask the following questions:

1. What was good about what each student said to (name of student who expressed unbelief)? *(Allow students to discuss. The first student's response was good because he was ready to give facts that would help prove creation. The second student's response was good because he made sure the student didn't feel disliked or left out. The third student's response was good because God may be the only one who can help change someone's mind.)*

2. What might have been bad about what each student said? *(The first student's response might have made the student feel stupid. The second student's response might have made him think that nothing was wrong with his not believing. The third response probably shouldn't have been said in front of the student and might make him feel mad or stupid.)*

Explain that although each response alone was not completely good, all three of them together make up a formula found in the Bible that tells us how to respond to faith challenges.

1. Look *up* to God to ask for help in responding to and praying for the person you are talking to. The student who wanted to pray was using this response. Ask students to get the red strips from the ceiling and place them in order. Read the first part of the verse together: "In your hearts set apart Christ as Lord."

Did You Know?
When the Bible was written thousands of years ago, people didn't understand how the sun and stars could make days, years, and seasons. The only way that information could be in the Bible (Genesis 1:14) is because God knew it was true! And now, thousands of years later, we have discovered that the Bible is exactly right—the sun does give us days, years, and seasons.

2. Look *down* to the Bible and other information and research. The student who talked about the Bible and science was using this response. Ask students to get the blue strips from the floor and place them in order below the first part of the verse. Read the first two parts of the verse together: "In your hearts set apart Christ as Lord. Always be prepared to give an answer to everyone to asks you to give the reason for the hope that you have."

3. Look *out* to consider how others feel and the example for Christ that you are setting. The student who promised to remain friends used this response. Ask students to get the yellow strips from the walls of the room and place them in order below the other strips. Read the verses together: "In your hearts set apart Christ as Lord. Always be prepared to give an answer to everyone who asks you to give the reason for the hope that you have. But do this with gentleness and respect, keeping a clear conscience, so that those who speak maliciously against your good behavior in Christ may be ashamed of their slander."

Step 4

Set up role play stations around the room. Place a card describing the role play on the table or wall and provide appropriate props, paper, and pencils. Ask students to work in pairs and choose three role plays to complete. At each role play, if necessary, they should do the role play two times, switching roles.

Materials
index cards with role plays written on them, paper, pencils, popcorn, cups, juice or water, science magazines, jar of pond water, index card with "Science Experiment" written on it

Role Play #1: You are taking a test. One question is: In what way do most people believe our world began? How will you look up, down, and out to stand up for your faith? *(Provide paper and pencils.)*

Role Play #2: You and your friend are snacking and watching a TV special about science. The narrator says that human beings are just another type of animal. Your friend laughs and says, "Yeah, all you need to do is look at our fifth grade class." How will you look up, down, and out to stand up for your faith? *(Provide bags of popcorn and cups of juice or water.)*

Role Play #3: You and your friend are reading an article in your favorite science magazine. It tells about a molecule some scientists made that was almost alive. The magazine says that we'll probably be able to create life someday soon. How will you look up, down, and out to stand up for your faith? *(Provide a kid's magazine such as 3-2-1 Contact or National Geographic World.)*

Role Play #4: You and your friend are doing a science project together on forms of life in pond water. You want to add a sentence to your project, telling about the impossible chance that even the life in a small drop of pond water would have happened by accident. Your friend says, "But that's religion, not science!" How will you look up, down, and out to stand up for your faith? *(Provide a jar of pond water, or something similar, and an index card with "Science Project" printed at the top.)*

When the student pairs have finished their role plays, gather in a large group and ask student volunteers to role play their responses for the class. Discuss the role plays and ask the following questions:

1. How did you feel about standing up for your faith? *(Maybe afraid to speak up, but afterwards good about speaking out.)*

2. Have you ever been in a situation where you needed to stand up for creation? How did you feel? What did you do? *(If possible, share one of your own experiences. Then encourage students to share.)*

Take It to the Next Level

Ask the students to stand in a circle. Place the puzzle pieces face down in the center of the circle. At your signal, ask the students to choose one or two puzzle pieces and go sit down in their place in the circle. Students should not show their puzzle pieces to anyone else. When each student has chosen a puzzle piece, go around the circle and ask each student to guess what they think the completed puzzle picture is.

After students have guessed, show them the picture on the front of the puzzle box. Explain that understanding our world is like a puzzle. We each learn pieces of the puzzle, but only God has the whole picture.

When scientists who believe in evolution spout important-sounding information, we need to remember that they are only holding a piece of the puzzle. In fact, God talks about wise-sounding people like that in the Bible. Read 1 Corinthians 3:18, 19a. The way we can be wise is to trust what God says!

Ask students to print something on the back of their puzzle piece that will help them remember to stand up for their faith. It could be a fact they learned about how God created the world. It could be the faith formula they learned. It could be a Bible verse they studied today!

When students are finished, ask volunteers to share what they wrote on their puzzle piece. Ask the students to take their puzzle pieces home to remind them that only God has the whole picture of creation!

Materials
a puzzle with fifty or fewer, fairly large pieces (Use a puzzle picture that has several different items in it so that the whole picture is not easily identifiable by one piece.)

Ask several students to close with prayer, asking God to help the group stand up for their faith!

Optional Activity

If your students need a break from heavy scientific knowledge, use the following experiment anytime during the session for some energy-releasing activity.

Spread the candy out onto a table. Have students stand around the table. Give each student a straw.

Explain to your students that any place that has no air in it is called a vacuum. When there is a vacuum, air rushes in to fill the empty space. That is why a vacuum cleaner sucks in air. Tell students they can create their own vacuum using a straw. They will suck out the air in the straw and cover the open end with a fingertip and then the end with their tongue to make a vacuum. Release the finger, hold the straw over a candy, and the air (and candy) will rush in to take its place. Ask students to use their vacuums to pick up pieces of candy. They only get to eat the candy they pick up with their vacuums. If you wish, have contests to see who can pick up the most pieces of candy in one minute.

Materials
straws, large bag of bite-size candy

Which model did I put together? How can you tell?

Which mobile shows people who worship the earth instead of God? Which mobile shows people who don't take care of the earth? Which mobile shows how God wants us to take care of the earth?

What is the way to God?

Name the Indian princess who became a Christian.

Write about a time when you stood up for your faith.

NO REFUND • NO EXCHANGE	NO REFUND • NO EXCHANGE	NO REFUND • NO EXCHANGE	NO REFUND • NO EXCHANGE	NO REFUND • NO EXCHANGE
ADMIT ONE	ADMIT ONE	ADMIT ONE	ADMIT ONE	ADMIT ONE
GENERAL ADMISSION	GENERAL ADMISSION	GENERAL ADMISSION	GENERAL ADMISSION	GENERAL ADMISSION
SEAT: G 17 GATE: A	SEAT: G 17 GATE: A	SEAT: G 17 GATE: A	SEAT: G 17 GATE: A	SEAT: G 17 GATE: A

Student #1 *(raise your hand)* "I don't really believe all this stuff about creation. I mean, all the scientists say the world evolved."

Student #2 *(jump right in to respond to the first student who speaks)* "But look at everything we just studied! It's not just that the Bible says the world was created, but science does not disprove what the Bible says. When you look at the evidence, how could you doubt creation?"

Student #3 "It's OK if you don't believe in creation. I mean, we're not going to kick you out of class or anything. You should be allowed to believe whatever you want."

Student #4 "Anyway, we're not going to change your mind by talking. I think we should all pray that God will help you believe."

Standing Up for the Earth God Gave Us

Memory Verse. 1 Peter 3:15, 16

Know man's role in caring for creation.
Feel confidence in responding to faith challenges.
Role play answers to those who worship or abuse the earth.

Before You Begin

It will be helpful if you do some homework before this session. Find out what environmental concerns are being taught in school. Notice what issues are currently in the media. Your students may be learning that our ozone layer is dangerously being depleted and our supply of oxygen is in danger because of diminishing rain forests. Although the focus of this session is not deciding whether these are valid concerns, it would be helpful for you to have information to balance the perspective they receive at school or from the media. Besides responding to these concerns, however, keep the focus on specific, local ways that they can care for the environment rather than on sweeping, general problems that can't be proved or solved in the classroom.

Get Into the Game

Before the session, set up the ticket booth as you did last week. Cut out the patterns from page 102. Punch a hole in the top of each figure. Make three mobiles by tying the figures together and then tying them to a hanger. Label the mobiles A, B, and C. The A mobile should have God at the top, then man, then the earth. The B mobile should have man at the top, then the earth. The C mobile should have the earth at the top and then man. Hang the mobiles near the ticket booth table.

As students arrive, have them take a ticket, write the answers to the questions, and put the tickets in the box. Students do not need to write their names on the tickets.

Materials

three photocopies of the patterns on page 102, hole punch, scissors, string, three hangers, photocopies of the ticket for Session 2 from page 95, the ticket booth sign used last session

Step 1

An adult will need to supervise each of these activities. Students should move in groups at specific times from one activity to the other rather than at random.

If you are the only leader, complete the activities as a large group. If time is limited, choose only one or two. If you have three adults, divide the students into three groups and have groups move from one activity to the next at your signal. You will need to provide supplies for the activity to be done three separate times for "Make a Water Filter" and "What's in a Rainstorm?"

Experiment #1—Make a Water Filter

Have an adult help you punch a few holes in the bottom of the plastic dish. Lay both coffee filters in the bottom of the dish. Put sand, then gravel in each coffee filter. Now set the dish in the glass bowl. Slowly pour the muddy water over the top of the gravel. Watch the water drain into the glass bowl. How does it look? What do you think happened to the mud and dirt?

Conclusion: The sand and rocks act as a natural filtering system to remove the dirt from the water. God made our world to work the same way to clean water. When rain falls, it filters through the earth and rocks, down to stream beds and rivers.

Materials

empty plastic container (such as a margarine or whipped cream tub), glass bowl, some gravel or small rocks, two coffee filters, sand, two cups of muddy water

Experiment #2—What's in a Rainstorm?

You may wish to perform this experiment in the kitchen. Using a stove or hot plate and a pan of water or an electric skillet with water in it, heat the water to boiling. Place about half of the ice cubes in the pie tin. Use the kitchen mitt to protect your hand and hold the tin of ice cubes over the boiling water. What appears on the bottom of the tin? What happens to the water drops when they get big enough?

Now remove the tin from the heat. Put the rest of the ice cubes in the tin. Add some green food coloring to the water in the pan and be sure it is mixed in well. Use the kitchen mitt and hold the tin over the water again. What appears on the bottom of the tin? What color are the rain drops?

Conclusion: What is in water comes down with the rain. If the water had chemicals or dirt in it, they would also be in the rain.

Materials

pie tin, bowl of ice cubes, stove, hot plate and pan of water or electric skillet with water in it, kitchen mitt, green food coloring

Experiment #3—God's Recycling Plan

Go for a walk outside and ask each student to choose one item of nature to bring back inside. Discuss what will happen to each item and its parts eventually. Examples follow: a leaf (eventually turns to dirt); a flower (seeds will grow other flowers and the rest will turn to dirt); a piece of wood (will rot and turn to dirt or will harden and become like stone). What happens to animals and people after they die? (They also turn to dirt.)

(Note: You may wish to gather a backup supply of natural items to use if weather doesn't permit a walk outside.)

Conclusion: Recycling was God's idea. He has had a recycling plan in place since He created the world. Imagine if God had not created a plan to get rid of leaves, wood, animals, and people. What a mess our world would be!

Step 2

Gather students in a large group. Open up the ticket box and read several of the answers on the tickets. (Mobile C shows people who worship the earth instead of God. Mobile B shows people who don't take care of the earth. Mobile A shows that God wants us to take care of the earth.) Ask students the following questions:

1. In each mobile, who is in charge? *(Mobile A—God is in charge. Mobile B—Man is in charge. Mobile C—The earth is in charge.)*

2. Why do some people abuse the earth by not taking care of it? *(They think they can do whatever they want to the earth because they're in charge.)*

3. There are some people who believe the earth is like God—they worship it. What might be wrong with how they treat the earth? *(They might think it is more important to take care of plants and animals than it is to take care of people or to worship God the Creator.)*

Ask students to turn to Genesis 1:26-30 in their Bibles to discover the role God gave man in creation. Read the verses together, then ask:

1. What was man's responsibility to the animals and to the plants? *(Man was to rule over fish, birds, and animals. God said that all the plants were given to him for food.)*

2. How do you think God intended for us to rule over the animals? *(Rule not only means that we are in charge, but we can also use them for work or for food. Rule also means that we are responsible for their food and their homes.)*

3. For what other reasons are plants important to us besides food? *(They provide us with oxygen. Their roots keep the soil in place so that the wind doesn't blow it to bare rock. They provide shade from the heat of the sun. Some provide medicines. Trees provide wood for paper, homes, furniture, and many other things.)* Explain that God had His own plan to care for the environment of the earth. Ask students to read Genesis 3:19 to

Materials
mobiles from opening activity, chalkboard and chalk or poster board and marker

Did You Know?
World Vision International, a Christian organization, has made caring for the environment part of their work in a valley in Ethiopia. They planted millions of trees to give food and fuel to the people, and they helped the people plant crops that need very little water. Now the valley is green, and the people grow enough food to send to other regions.

find a clue to part of God's plan. Then discuss what the students discovered in Experiments #1 and #3 at the beginning of the session. *(God has a natural plan for cleaning water that soaks into the ground. God also has a plan to get rid of dying trees, plants, animals, and people.)*

Explain that God already has a plan to keep our environment healthy. Part of our job in caring for the environment is to make sure that God's plan is not hurt by man's work. *(Discuss what the students discovered about rain in the second activity.)*

Ask students to name some environmental concerns. Encourage them to think of things they have heard at school, read in books or magazines, or seen on TV. Make a list of issues the students name. Then divide the students into three groups. One group will believe the earth and the environment are like God—they worship the earth. Another group will believe that man is completely in charge of the earth. Another group will believe that God gave man a responsibility to care for the earth. Choose some of the issues from the list and give the groups a minute or two to discuss what their responses would be. Then ask each group to tell how they would respond. Be sure students know it's OK if groups agree on some issues. After students have responded to two or three issues, switch the group's roles so that a different group is worshiping, abusing, or caring for the earth.

Step 3

Take three pieces of poster board and print the following on each one:

1. "In your hearts set apart Christ as Lord."

2. "Always be prepared to give an answer to everyone who asks you to give a reason for the hope that you have."

3. "But do this with gentleness and respect, keeping a clear conscience, so that those who speak maliciously against your good behavior in Christ may be ashamed of their slander."

Ask the students to find 1 Peter 3:15, 16 in their Bibles. Read the verses together, then ask these questions:

1. What are the three parts of our faith formula that are found in these verses? *(Look up to God; look down to read information; look out to others.)*

2. What two things can we ask God when we look to Him? *(For help in knowing what to say; to pray for the person we are talking to.)*

3. Where can we look down to find information about the faith challenge? *(First, to the Bible; then to other information and research, such as scientific information.)*

4. What two things should we be thinking about when we

Materials
three pieces of poster board

look out at others? (*How they are feeling about our response; what kind of example we are setting for Christ.*)

Divide the students into three groups. Give each group one of the pieces of poster board. As you randomly call out *up, down,* or *out,* the appropriate group should stand and say that part of the verse. When students are comfortable saying their part of the verse, practice reciting the verses together.

Step 4

Materials
index cards, Bible, snacks (Gummi Bears, Fruit Roll Ups, etc.)

Set up the role plays in different areas of the room as you did last session. Print the instructions on a card and provide any listed props in each area. Students can work in groups of two or three to complete the role plays. Students should complete at least three role plays.

Role Play #1: You and your friend are at the mall, and you ask if she wants to stop and get a hamburger. Your friend says, "No, I'm not eating meat any more. I don't think it's right to kill animals." How can you look up, down, and out to stand up for your faith? (*Hint: Read Genesis 1:28; 3:21; 4:4.*)

Role Play #2: You and your friend are walking home from school, and your friends throws his candy wrapper on the ground. When you walk back to pick it up, he says, "Just leave it. No one's gonna know who left it there anyway." How can you look up, down, and out to stand up for your faith? (*Provide small packs of Gummi Bears, Fruit Roll Ups, or some other snack.*)

Role Play #3: Your class is starting a unit on caring for the environment. Your teacher asks, "Can anybody tell me some reasons why it is important to take care of our earth?" How can you look up, down, and out to stand up for your faith?

Role Play #4: You are with a group of friends in the woods behind your house, and you find a stray cat. Your friends want to throw rocks at the cat and torture it in other ways. How can you look up, down, and out to stand up for your faith?

When the students are finished, gather in a large group and have student volunteers role-play their answers to the situations. Discuss the role plays and ask:

1. Which role play was the hardest for you? Why?

2. Have you ever had to stand up for your faith concerning an environmental issue? Tell us about it. (*Share a personal experience and encourage students to do the same.*)

Take It to the Next Level

Materials
photocopies of page 102, scissors, yarn or string, hole punch, wire hangers, markers or colored pencils

Explain to the students that they will make their own mobile to remind them of their place in caring for God's creation.

Distribute the materials. The students should cut out the three figures, color them, punch a hole in the top of each, and attach them to the hangers, with God at the top, then man, then the earth.

When the students have completed their mobiles, ask them to print something on the backs of the figures that will remind them to stand up for the role God gave man in caring for the environment. On the figure representing God, they could print a Scripture concerning what God says about caring for the earth. They could print an environmental concern on the earth. On the figure of the man, they could write what they will do about the concern they chose.

Optional Activity

If your students need an active break anytime during the session, use the following activity. It's guaranteed to use up gallons of excess energy.

Explain to the students that one of the reasons Americans are concerned about water is because of how much we use! In a country without running water, a person carrying water home every day uses only three to four gallons a day. But the average American uses about fifty gallons of water a day. Tell your students that they will discover how big a difference that is.

Ask the students to crumple up newspaper into balls to fill the gallon jugs. Time how long it takes them to fill the jugs. Then ask them to crumple up newspaper to fill the trash cans. Time how long it takes them. Compare to the difference in amounts of water this would be.

If you have time, discuss how the students could save water and have them scoop out a few gallons of newspaper each time they name a way to save (e.g., take shorter showers, turn off the water when brushing teeth, drink refrigerated cold water instead of waiting for tap water to run cold, water the lawn less often).

Materials
three or four empty gallon milk containers with the tops cut off of them, two empty trash cans, a stack of old newspapers

Mobile Patterns

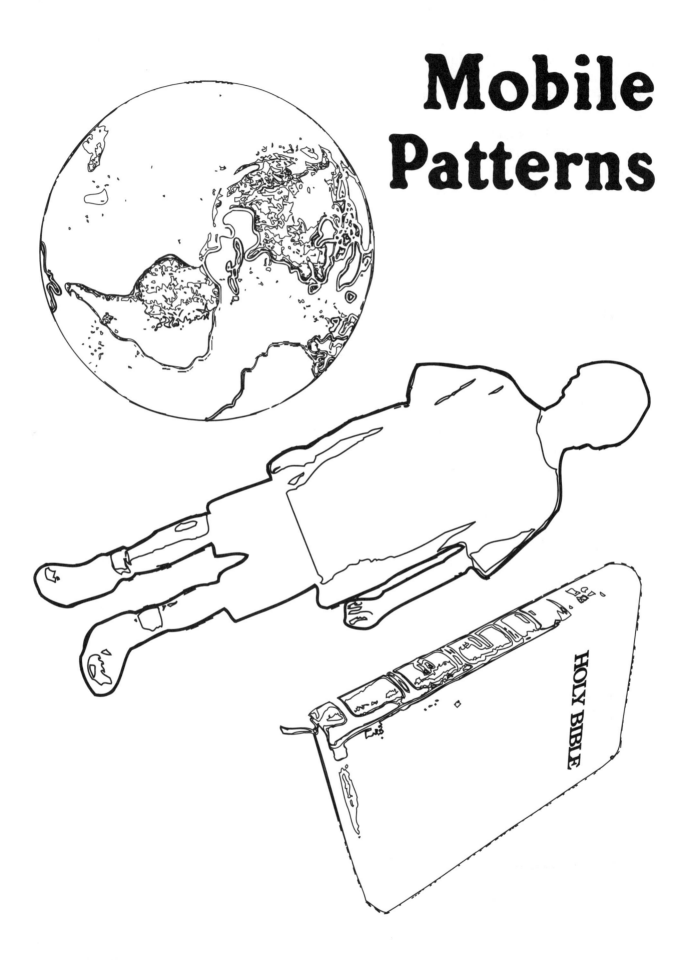

Standing Up for Jesus

Memory Verse. 1 Peter 3:15, 16

Know that the only way to God is through Jesus.
Feel confident in their ability to respond to faith challenges.
Role play answers to those who question Jesus as the way to God.

Before You Begin

Provide information relating to specific challenges your students face concerning their faith in Jesus. Is there a large population of Buddhists or Muslims in your area? Do your students know people who believe in crystals or astrology? Perhaps you feel your students are influenced more by the philosophies they see in the cartoons or TV shows they watch every day. Work hard to focus on ideas your students come into contact with daily, rather than abstract philosophies that they only read or hear about.

The book, *Faith Training,* includes two related chapters, one on the uniqueness of Jesus and the other on world religions and cults. The information provides a great resource for this session.

Get Into the Game

As students arrive, have them take a ticket, write the answers to the question, and put the tickets in the box. Students do not need to write their names on the tickets.

Materials

photocopies of the ticket for Session 3 from page 95, the ticket booth sign used for the last two sessions

Step 1

Set up booths in different areas of the room, or if possible, outside different rooms in your building. Each booth will represent a way people try to get to God. You will need to have an adult at each booth. Make a large sign and place it in a prominent place as students enter the room: This Way to God. Point arrows in all different directions on the sign. Explain to students as they arrive that they should visit each of the booths to see if they can find the way to God.

For each booth, you will need a table and chair, a poster board sign that says, "The Way to God," a flashlight, and a

Materials

"This Way to God" sign, three of the following: table, chair, "The Way to God" sign, flashlight, booth small booth (large enough for one student) or a separate room. Suggestions for the booths: a refrigerator box, taped shut, with a doorway cut in it for students to enter; small stand-alone tent; two tables placed on their sides with a blanket thrown over them.

Booth #1

You will need photocopies of the top of page 110, pencils, and a sign that says, "Wrong Way!" in large letters.

Before students arrive, tape the "Wrong Way!" sign somewhere inside the booth.

As students arrive at the booth, give them the reproducible page. With a bored, disinterested expression, tell them to check one or more names, and they can enter. As students turn in their papers, they may enter one at a time with the flashlight.

Booth #2

You will need a small balance scale (a small kitchen scale will work if a balance scale is not available), a timer, a large stack of pennies, and a sign that says, "Wrong Way!" in large letters, and in smaller letters, "All people have sinned and are not good enough for God's glory" (Romans 3:23, *ICB).* "He saved us because of his mercy, not because of good deeds we did to be right with God" (Titus 3:5, *ICB).*

Before students arrive, tape the, "Wrong Way!" sign somewhere inside the booth.

As students arrive at the booth, tell each student he has thirty seconds to name bad things he has done, and thirty seconds to name good things he has done. Set the timer. Place a penny on one side of the scale for every bad thing named and on the other side of the scale for every good thing named. (If you are using a kitchen scale, weigh bad and good things separately.) When a student is finished, compare to see which side of the scale wins—good or bad. If by some chance the bad scale outweighs the good, wave the child on through. Say, "It's OK, go on through. After all, you didn't kill anybody or anything like that."

Booth #3

You will need photocopies of the bottom of page 110, pencils, and a sign that says, "Wrong Way!" in large letters, and in smaller letters, "For since the creation of the world God's invisible qualities—his eternal power and divine nature—have been clearly seen, being understood from what has been made, so that men are without excuse" (Romans 1:20).

Before students arrive, tape the sign inside the booth.

As students arrive at the booth, ask them to check one or

Materials
photocopies of page 110, pencils, sign, tape

Materials
small balance scale or small kitchen scale, timer, large stack of pennies, sign, tape

Materials
photocopies of page 110, pencils, sign, tape

two reasons on the reproducible page, then let them go through one at a time.

Step 2

Gather students in a large group, then ask the following questions:

1. What are some ways to God that you named on your tickets or found on the booth? *(Open up the ticket box and read some of the tickets. Let students discuss their experiences in the booths.)*

2. Some people believe there are many ways to God, and it doesn't matter which one you choose. Who are the people named at the booth? Who are other people or things people believe in to try to get to God? *(The Mormons believe Joseph Smith; some people worship the sun or other natural objects to get to God; some people think they are a part of God or are God, so if they understand themselves better, they'll know God better.)*

3. What is wrong with believing there are a lot of ways to God? *(Let students respond.)* Ask a student to go get the "Wrong Way!" sign from Booth #1. Read together Acts 4:10, 12. Explain that the Bible makes it extremely clear that the only way to God is through Jesus. Ask students to find John 14:6. Read the verse together. What way is Jesus talking about? *(The way to God. Jesus is the only way to God.)*

4. Some people believe they can get to God by being good enough and not doing too many bad things. Ask students to think of some movies, TV shows, or books in which someone supposedly went to Heaven or talked about going to Heaven because they were a good person. *(Let students respond.)*

If possible, before the session set up the video of a movie you know your students are familiar with and cue it to a place that talks about or depicts what happens after death. Some movies that deal with this subject are: any of the *Star Wars* trilogy, *Casper, The Lion King.*

What is wrong with the idea that people can be good so that they go to Heaven? *(Let students respond.)* Ask a student to get the "Wrong Way!" sign from Booth #2. Read together the Scriptures (Romans 3:23; Titus 3:5). Explain that none of us is good. We have all done wrong things. That's the reason we needed Jesus to die for the wrong things we do. He didn't die for us because God decided we were good enough; He died because God loved us!

Some people think the easiest way to God is to ignore Him for a long time and make excuses forever. They think that God is so loving that He will accept their excuses. Ask students to

Did You Know?
Other religions are different from Christianity in five ways: 1. They don't believe Jesus is who He said He was; 2. They elevate someone to a higher spiritual position than he or she deserves; 3. They add new information or another religious work to the Bible; 4. They do not believe in the unity of God the Father, God the Son, and God the Holy Spirit; 5. They do not believe we are saved totally by grace. (Adapted from *Faith Training* by Joe White, Ed.D.)

list some reasons that they've heard friends or other adults give for not worrying about God. (Students can list some of the excuses on the page they filled out at the booth, and other excuses they've heard.)

What is wrong with the idea that we can excuse our choices to God? *(Let students respond.)* Ask a student to get the "Wrong Way!" sign from Booth #3. Read the Scripture together (Romans 1:20). Explain that we have no excuse for not believing what God says. We have already discovered that He says the only way to Him is through Jesus. But the Bible talks even more about excuses. Jesus tells a story about some men who made excuses. Ask students to find Luke 14:15-24 in their Bibles. Explain that the story is about a man who invited people to a banquet. Can you find the three excuses the men made? *(I bought a field. I bought a yoke of oxen. I just got married.)* Read verse 24. What happened to the men who made excuses? *(They wouldn't even get a taste of the banquet.)* Explain that Jesus was comparing the man who gave the banquet to God. The men who were invited are just like us. God won't accept excuses from us, just as the man wouldn't accept excuses for his banquet.

Step 3

You may complete this activity in the kitchen, or mix the cookies in your classroom and have an adult helper take them to the kitchen to bake.

Before the session, place the pre-measured ingredients in separate containers. (Ziploc plastic bags work well for the dry ingredients. The eggs and vanilla could be put in small, sealable plastic containers.) On the outside of each container, tape a strip of paper with a section of the memory verse on it. Tape the strips in order, so that when the students place the ingredients in the order given, the verse words will be in order. Divide the verse as follows: In your hearts set apart Christ as Lord; Always be prepared to give an answer; to everyone who asks you; to give the reason for the hope that you have; But do this with gentleness and respect; keeping a clear conscience; so that those who speak maliciously; against your good behavior in Christ; may be ashamed of their slander.

Set the ingredients in random order on a table or counter.

Explain to the students that when you make chocolate chip cookies, it is important to include all the ingredients. What do you think would happen if we left out the flour? the baking soda? the eggs? *(Too runny; very flat; too dry and crumbly.)* Tell students that using the faith formula in 1 Peter is like making chocolate chip cookies—it is important to include all the

Materials

ingredients for chocolate chip cookies— 1 cup margarine, ¾ cup sugar, ¾ cup brown sugar, 2 eggs, 1 tsp. vanilla, 1 tsp. baking soda, 1 tsp. salt, 2½ cups flour, 2 cups chocolate chips; a mixing bowl; spoon; baking sheet.

ingredients. What might happen if we weren't prepared to give an answer? if we didn't answer with gentleness and respect? if we hadn't set Christ as Lord? *(We wouldn't be able to respond and might look stupid; we might make people angry and unwilling to listen about God again; we wouldn't have the help of God's Spirit in changing people's attitudes and hearts.)*

Tell students that in order to make the chocolate chip cookies correctly, they need to place the memory verse phrases in order. Let students work together to accomplish this. Then add the ingredients in order, one at a time, letting different volunteers add and stir the ingredients. As you are working, discuss the verses and ask these questions:

1. Can you name the two reasons that we look up to God for help? *(To pray for the other person; to pray for help for us as we talk.)*

2. What can we study to be prepared to give an answer? *(Most importantly—God's Word, but also scientific evidence, history, or other research that relates to what we're talking about.)*

3. When we look out to others, what should we be thinking about ourselves? What should we be thinking about them? *(We should be concerned about setting a good example for Christ. We should also be concerned about their feelings.)*

When the cookies are mixed, have an adult helper bake them at 375 degrees for 8-10 minutes, while you and the students continue with other activities. The helper should be prepared to bring the cookies back to class during **Take It to the Next Level.**

Step 4

Set up the role plays in different areas of the room as you did in the last two sessions. Print the instructions on a card and provide any listed props in each area. Students can work in groups of two or three to complete the role plays.

Role Play #1: Your friend knows you go to church and believe in God. He says, "Our new next door neighbors believe in God too. They are Muslims." How can you look up, down, and out to stand up for your faith? *(Provide an "M" encyclopedia, preferably a children's encyclopedia. Be sure it has an entry under Muslims. If not, check under Islam and change the role play directions to reflect this.)*

Role Play #2: You invite your friend to go to church with you. Your friend says, "I can't right now. Maybe I will when soccer season is over." How can you look up, down, and out to stand up for your faith? *(Provide a soccer ball.)*

Role Play #3: Your great-grandma just died, and she is in Heaven because she believed in Jesus. Your friend's mom

Materials
index cards with situations written on them, children's encyclopedia, soccer ball

says, "I'm sorry your great-grandma died, but I'm sure she's in Heaven. She was such a good person!" How can you look up, down, and out to stand up for your faith?

When the students are finished, gather in a large group and have student volunteers role-play their answers. Then discuss the role plays.

Ask students, "Have you ever had to stand up for your faith in Jesus? Tell us about it." Share a personal experience. Then encourage students to share.

Take It to the Next Level

Materials
video or recording of "I'm Not Ashamed" by Newsboys (Check to see if your Christian bookstore has this song on video available for rental.), poster board, markers, and notes to send home with students explaining that they have designed a T-shirt logo and can order T-shirts at a certain price

Before the session, find a place in your area that will print T-shirts and ask for a cost estimate to place on the note you send home.

Ask the students, "How does the memory verse say people will feel if we answer with gentleness and respect?" (*ashamed of their slander*)

"The way we answer others should make those who criticize us feel ashamed. But we should feel exactly the opposite of that—Not Ashamed!" Ask students to find Romans 1:16 in their Bibles. Read the verse aloud together.

"What are some ways you can show you are not ashamed?" (Let students respond.)

Tell students that one easy way they can stand up is by wearing something that tells about their faith. Ask them to work together to design a T-shirt logo on the poster board. The logo could say "Not Ashamed" or "I'm Not Ashamed." It could have Romans 1:16 on it. It could have "Ashamed" at the top, crossed out with "Not!" printed below it. Let the students use their creativity and imagination in their design. Students may munch on chocolate chip cookies made during Step 3 as they work. When the students are done, tell them they will have an opportunity to order a T-shirt with their design on it and give them the notes to take home.

Close by playing the recording or showing the video of "I'm Not Ashamed" by Newsboys.

If it is not possible for you to order T-shirts, choose one of the following options.

1. Have each student design a small poster (half a sheet of poster board) to take home and hang in his room.

2. Provide plain T-shirts and fabric paint. (Or send a note home after Session 2, asking each student to bring a plain T-shirt to class.) Have each student create his own logo on the T-shirt using the fabric paint.

Optional Activity

Use this activity anytime during the session when the students need an active break. Play the recording of "I'm Not Ashamed." Ask the students to make up a routine to the song. The students can do a simple repetitive action such as clapping hands or snapping fingers during the verses, and make up actions to do during the chorus.

If you have a video camera available, make a video of the students' completed choreography. You can play the video during **Bridge the Gap**, which the parents will attend.

Materials
recording of "I'm Not Ashamed" by Newsboys

✔Ways to God?

___ Muhammad

___ Buddha

___ Jesus

___ Confucius

___ Sun Myung Moon

___ Joseph Smith

___ Mary Baker Eddy

___ Myself

___ Other (List names below)

_____

_____

_____

✔Why have you not found God?

Check one or more reasons why you have not found the way to God.

___ Not enough time.

___ It's too confusing.

___ I don't care.

___ No one told me the way.

___ I'm too young to worry about it right now.

___ There is no God.

Standing Up for the U.S.A.

Memory Verse. 1 Peter 3:15, 16

Know that the U.S.A. was founded by men of faith.
Feel confident in their ability to respond to faith challenges.
Prepare an answer to those who deny our heritage of faith.

Before You Begin

As you review sample history books from school or public libraries, you might discover that many texts downplay or completely leave out the role that faith in God played in the founding of the United States of America. This session provides small bits taken from the large amount of information on this topic. It would be helpful to have the resources listed on pages 7 and 8 available for your students to read or take home. The principles apply to any nation.

Get Into the Game

Set up the ticket booth. As students arrive, have them take a ticket, write the answer to the question, and put the tickets in the box. Students do not need to write their names on the tickets.

Materials

photocopies of the ticket for Session 4 from page 95, the ticket booth sign used for the last three sessions

Step 1

These activities will work best if you divide the students into three groups and have them move at a given signal from activity to activity. Be sure to provide three sheets of poster board for the activity, "The Real Story of Pocahontas," so each group will have one. If you only have leaders for two groups, you could provide the activity, "The Secret of My Success," as an extra center that students could go to if they finish early at one of the other activities.

Activity #1—One Country's Motto

Ask students to look up the word "motto" in the dictionary. Discuss what a motto is. Ask students to think of mottoes they have heard (companies often use mottoes in commercials; schools and other organizations often have mottoes).

Ask students to decide what the country's motto should be

Materials

dictionary, some coins and various denominations of bills, a copy of "The Star-Spangled Banner" (most hymnals contain the national anthem), an American flag by looking at the money, the National Anthem, and the Pledge of Allegiance.

Activity #2—The Real Story of Pocahontas

Ask the students to answer the questions about the pretend Pocahontas. They can use the encyclopedia to help them answer the questions about the real Pocahontas on the reproducible page.

1. How old was Pocahontas when she met John Smith? *(pretend, around 18; real, 12 or 13)*

2. Who did Pocahontas fall in love with? *(pretend, John Smith; real, John Rolfe)*

3. Who do you think Pocahontas believed was God? *(pretend, the earth; real, the one, true God)*

When the students have answered the questions, ask them to use this information to work together to write and illustrate the real story of Pocahontas on the poster board.

Materials
an encyclopedia, photocopies of page 117, a large piece of poster board, colored pencils or markers (optional: You may wish to provide a VCR and a copy of the movie *Pocahontas.*)

Activity #3—The Secret of Success

Explain that the United States is one of the most successful nations on earth. It is a good place to live.

Ask the students, "What are some things that you think make the country successful? What are some things that make the country a good place to live?" *(Let students respond. Some ideas: freedom of religion, system of government, belief in God, wealth of food and resources compared to the rest of the world.)*

Ask students to make a poster of things that make the country successful and a good place to live. They can draw or write their own ideas or cut them out of the magazines and newspapers and glue them on the poster board.

Materials
poster board, scissors, glue, a variety of old magazines or newspapers

Step 2

Gather students in a large group. Open up the ticket box and read several of the answers on the tickets.

If they do not already know it, tell students the correct answer *(Pocahontas)*. Ask the students who wrote the real story of Pocahontas to share it with the large group. Explain that there are many other familiar names in the country's history who were dedicated Christians and men of God. Read the following clues to the students and ask them to guess the answer. Allow students to try to guess after Clue #1; then read Clue #2.

Clue #1: He said, "The fact that the gospel must still be preached to so many lands in such a short time . . . this is what convinces me."

Clue #2: He is credited with discovering the continent of America.
(Answer: Christopher Columbus)

Clue #1: Their first act upon reaching the American shore was to kneel down and thank God.

Clue #2: They sailed on a ship called the Mayflower.
(Answer: Pilgrims)

Clue #1: When all the men were fighting and could not agree about what should be in the United States Constitution, he suggested that they go home to pray.

Clue #2: He used a kite to "discover" electricity.
(Answer: Benjamin Franklin)

Clue #1: He urged his countrymen to fight for freedom by saying, "There is a just God who presides over the destinies of nations; and who will raise up friends to fight our battles for us."

Clue #2: He said, "Give me liberty or give me death!"
(Answer: Patrick Henry)

Clue #1: A soldier found him on his knees in the snow, praying to God for his country.

Clue #2: He was the first president of the United States.
(Answer: George Washington)

Clue #1: He was the first president to live in the White House. He asked that God would bless it and prayed, "May none but Honest and Wise Men ever rule under this Roof."

Clue #2: He was the second president of the United States.
(Answer: John Adams)

Explain that the faith of these men and women greatly influenced what they believed would make the country successful. "Do Americans live in a successful country? Why or why not?" *(Allow students to discuss. Ask students to share some of the items they put on the poster during Step 1.)*

"Why do you think our country was and is successful?" *(Allow students to give ideas.)*

Explain that the nation's forefathers believed that obeying God was the single, most important factor in having a successful nation. Review some of the items discussed in the clues: George Washington prayed for God's help in battle; Patrick Henry said God would send friends to help us; Benjamin Franklin asked that delegates pray for God's help in writing the Constitution; John Adams prayed for God's blessing on the White House.

Did You Know?
President Eisenhower added the words "under God" to the Pledge of Allegiance in 1954 after hearing a sermon concerning Abraham Lincoln's Gettysburg Address that talked about one nation "under God."

"Where did these men get the idea that God would bless their nation?" Accept students' ideas. Then ask students to find Psalm 33:12-19 and Proverbs 14:34 in their Bibles. Read the verses together. "What is the secret of a successful nation?" *(A nation that trusts and obeys God will be successful, no matter how strong they are.)*

"Look at the two Scriptures again. What are some things in these verses that would make a country and its people successful? What are some things that are found in these verses that contribute to a country's downfall?" *(Allow students to share their ideas. Help your students reach the conclusion that it is not money, knowledge, resources, or form of government that make us successful. It is trust and obedience to God.)*

"How can we follow the example of those founding fathers to help build a successful nation?" *(Let students respond. We can do our part by trusting and obeying God and by encouraging our friends and family to do the same. We can speak up about the country's history of faith, and we can speak up about laws that we think will help the country follow God.)*

Step 3

Before the session, attach a piece of masking tape to each ball. Write on the masking tape to label the balls "up," "down," and "out." On the chalkboard or poster board print:

1. Up: In your hearts set apart Christ as Lord.

2. Down: Always be prepared to give an answer to everyone who asks you to give the reason for the hope that you have.

3. Out: But do this with gentleness and respect, keeping a clear conscience, so that those who speak maliciously against your good behavior in Christ may be ashamed of their slander.

Ask the students to stand in a circle. Review 1 Peter 3:15, 16 by quoting it together. Then help students review the three steps to the faith formula by playing a game. Give three different students one of the balls. The "up" ball should be thrown through the air to another student. The "down" ball should be rolled on the floor to another student. The "out" ball should be bounce-passed to another student. (You may need to demonstrate each of these passes for the students.) As each student catches a ball, he should quote that part of the memory block. Then pass the balls to other students. Students may look at the parts of the memory block you have written on the chalkboard or poster board if they need help. At your signal, the three students should pass their balls simultaneously. For a fun warm-up, time the students to see how long they can keep the three balls moving without stopping.

Materials
three softballs, masking tape, chalkboard and chalk or poster board and marker

Did You Know?
When George Washington was inaugurated as the first President of the United States, he swore allegiance to the Constitution with his left hand upon the open Bible, resting on the Scripture, Genesis 49:22-25. Every U.S. President since Washington has been inaugurated with his hand on the Bible, opened to one of his favorite Scriptures.

Step 4

Set up the role plays in different areas of the room as in the last three sessions. Print the instructions on a card and provide any listed props in each area. Students can work in groups of two or three to complete the role plays.

Role Play #1: Your neighborhood park usually sets up a Christmas nativity scene every year. Now some people are protesting. Your friend says, "Well, I believe in God and everything, but in our country we don't have the right to push that onto other people." How can you look up, down, and out to stand up for your faith?

Role Play #2: Your teacher is telling you about the First Thanksgiving. She says the Pilgrims made a meal together with the Indians because they were thankful for the help the Indians had given them. How can you look up, down, and out to stand up for your faith?

Role Play #3: You have an assignment at school—write a paper about what makes the country great. How can you look up, down, and out to stand up for your faith? *(Provide paper and pencils.)*

When the students are finished, gather in a large group and have student volunteers role-play their responses. Ask students to share what they wrote for Role Play #3.

"Have you had a chance to stand up for your faith in the past few weeks? What did you say? How did you use the faith formula?" *(If possible, tell about a time when you recently stood up for your faith. Encourage students to share.)*

Materials
index cards with role plays written on them, paper, pencils

Take It to the Next Level

Ask students to cut out and glue the Scripture verse to one side of their index card. They should glue the Faith Formula Reminders from page 118 to the other side of their cards. They can decorate their cards as they wish. Then cover the cards with clear, adhesive-backed plastic. Punch a hole in the corner of each card. Students can tie rick rack or ribbon through the hole to make a loop. Encourage the students to place the card on their key chain, tie it to one of the rings of their notebook, or put it in some other prominent place that will help them remember to stand up for their faith.

Gather students in a large group. Hold hands and recite 1 Peter 3:15, 16 together. Then ask students to pray silently for the courage to stand up for Jesus as you play the song, "I'm Not Ashamed." Close with a short prayer, asking for God's wisdom and strength for your students.

Materials
index cards, photocopies of page 118, scissors, markers, glue, clear adhesive-backed plastic, paper hole punch, rick rack or ribbon, and a recording of "I'm Not Ashamed" (used in Session 3)

Optional Activity

Use the following game anytime during the session when your students need a break.

Play a "Jenga" type game using rectangular-shaped vanilla and chocolate wafer cookies. Have students make a tower out of the wafers by laying three across vertically, then three on top of those horizontally, and so on. Make at least fifteen layers. Divide students into three or four teams. Teams can take turns removing one cookie from any layer but the top layer. They should then place the cookie on top to continue building the tower. Let teams continue until the tower topples. Offer fresh cookies for a snack.

Explain that our country was built on a solid foundation of faith, and that faith made it successful. When we start trying to take away parts of that foundation, the country gets weaker and weaker, until it finally topples, like the cookie tower did.

Materials
rectangular-shaped vanilla and chocolate wafer cookies

Did You Know?
The First Amendment to our Constitution, protecting religious freedom, was added by James Madison, our fourth President. The amendment was added in response to a state-controlled church, such as the state of Virginia tried to have, in which no Baptists, Methodists, Lutherans, or any denomination other than Anglicans were allowed to follow their faith.

Who Was the Real Pocahontas?

	Pretend Pocahontas	Real Pocahontas
• How old was Pocahontas when she met John Smith?		
• Who did Pocahontas fall in love with?		
• Who do you think Pocahontas believed was God?		

Faith Formula

"In your hearts set apart Christ as Lord. Always be prepared to give an answer to everyone who asks you to give a reason for the hope that you have. But do this with gentleness and respect, keeping a clear conscience, so that those who speak maliciously against your good behavior in Christ may be ashamed of their slander."

—1 Peter 3:15, 16

Please help me know what to say.

Please help the person to listen.

What does the Bible say?

What does other research say?

Am I gentle and respectful?

Am I setting a good example for Christ?

Bridge the Gap

Standing Up for Our Faith

Memory Verse. 1 Peter 3:15, 16

Examine Scriptures and other research and evidence that will enable them to respond to faith challenges.

Feel confident in their ability to respond to faith challenges.

Prepare answers to four faith challenges.

This session is intended for your students and their parents. It offers a tremendous opportunity to challenge parents and give them the resources to continue teaching at home. If you have parents with younger children, it would be helpful to have a teen or other adult present in another area of the building as a baby-sitter.

See the Book Fair suggestion on the unit pages. It is likely that few parents would find time to go to a bookstore and look up the resources. Your students and their parents will benefit if you have the resources available at this session. Notify parents ahead of time, so they can be prepared to purchase what they want. Be sure to allow time at the beginning and end of the session for parents to look at the resources.

Get Into the Game

Before the session, set up the ticket booth as you have the last four sessions. As students and parents arrive, have them take a ticket. Tell them to describe their experience in three or four short sentences. They do not need to write their names on the tickets.

Step 1

Before the session, choose one lab activity from each of the first four sessions and set up the activities, providing the needed

Materials
photocopy of the ticket for Bridge the Gap from page 95, pens or pencils, the ticket booth sign used for the sessions

Materials
copies of the resources used in Sessions 1–4, Bibles, a camcorder, a blank video tape, a TV and VCR to play the recorded video (If you do not have a camcorder available, make a tape recording instead.)

119

supplies and instructions. Choose activities that will allow students and parents to move freely from activity to activity instead of being divided into four groups. Suggestions for activities are: "The Right Spin" from Session 1, "God's Recycling Plan" from Session 2, "Booth #1" from Session 3, and "The Secret of Our Success" from Session 4.

As students and parents arrive, encourage them to visit each of the four activities in any order they wish. Ask students to help explain the activities to their parents, if needed.

Step 2

Gather in a large group. Briefly explain what you and the students have been learning about standing up for our faith in regards to creation, the environment, Jesus, and the country's history. Explain that students and parents gain confidence to stand up for their faith when they have knowledge about the topic.

Divide into groups of six to eight people and distribute photocopies of the reproducible page.

Assign each group one of the topics covered in the first four sessions—God's creation of the world, caring for the environment, Jesus as the only way to God, and the heritage of faith for a country. Ask each group to work together to fill in "Standing Up for ____" using the Bible, the resources, and the knowledge and ideas of its members. Encourage groups to be creative. If groups need help, explain the sections. In "We believe," groups should put together a short summary of their belief concerning the topic. For example, "We believe that God created the world in six days." In "Did you know?" groups can put interesting facts from science or history or other resources that support their belief. In "The Bible says" groups should write out Scriptures that support their belief. In the blank boxes, groups can put a quote, a short statement about their topic, a key word about their topic, or a picture or symbol about their topic.

As the groups work on their fact sheets, go around the room with a video camera. At each group, stop and ask families to respond to these questions:

1. What do you believe about (the group's assigned topic)?
2. What interesting facts do you know about the topic?
3. What does the Bible say?

Encourage families to keep their responses short. If groups finish while you are still videotaping, allow them to browse at the Book Fair.

When all the groups have finished, rewind and play the videotape for the entire group.

Materials
photocopies of page 124, Bibles, video camera, TV, VCR

Step 3

Before the session, tape the cardboard box shut. Print instructions on each of the six sides of the box.

1. Say the "up" part of the verses.
2. Say the "down" part of the verses.
3. Say the "out" part of the verses.
4. What two things do you pray when you look up?
5. What two things do you study when you look down?
6. What two things do you remember when you look out?

Print the three sections of the memory block on poster board or chalkboard and label them Up, Down, and Out.

Up: In your hearts set apart Christ as Lord.

Down: Always be prepared to give an answer to everyone who asks you to give a reason for the hope that you have.

Out: But do this with gentleness and respect, keeping a clear conscience, so that those who speak maliciously against your good behavior in Christ may be ashamed of their slander.

Explain to the parents that the memory verses for the unit are found in 1 Peter 3:15, 16. Ask the group to read the verses aloud together from the poster board or chalkboard. Explain that the students have learned a faith formula from the memory verses that helps them when they stand up for their faith. Encourage students to share the formula by asking the following questions:

1. What are the three parts of our faith formula that are found in these verses? *(Look up to God; look down to read information; look out to others.)*

2. What two things can we ask God for when we look to Him? *(for help in knowing what to say; to pray for the person we are talking to)*

3. Where can we look down to find information about the faith challenge? *(first, to the Bible; then to other information and research, such as scientific information)*

4. What two things should we be thinking about when we look out at others? *(how they are feeling about our response; what kind of example we are setting for Christ)*

Play a game using the cardboard box you prepared before class. Students and parents can play in the same groups they were in for the "What Do We Believe?" time. Groups take turns rolling the box on the floor and following the instructions on the side of the box that lands face up. Groups can read the portions of the verses from the poster board or chalkboard, but encourage them to try to say parts of the verses without looking.

Materials
cardboard box, tape, marker, chalkboard and chalk or poster board and marker

Step 4

Materials
completed tickets from the ticket booth,
photocopies of page 123, resources

You will need the filled-out tickets from the ticket booth, photocopies of "Passing Your Faith Along," and resources that will
help groups research their responses to the situations on the
page. For example, an "M" encyclopedia, a book on the
Mormon faith, a book discussing George Washington's spiritual
life (the history book recommended on the unit pages does
this), a book with scientific facts about creation.

Choose several tickets that were filled out at the ticket booth
and read how students or parents stood up for their faith.
Encourage others to share times they stood up for their faith.

Work in the same groups used in the last two activities. Give
each group a photocopy of "Passing Your Faith Along" and
assign them one of the situations. Each group should be prepared to present the situation for the entire group.

When the groups are ready, have them present their situations. When they have finished, discuss their responses.

1. How did you feel about speaking up for your faith?
(Speaking up can be hard even in a friendly situation.)

2. Have you ever been in a situation like this? What happened?

Take It to the Next Level

Materials
memory block poster board or chalkboard from Step 3, a recording of "I'm
Not Ashamed" (used in Sessions 3 and 4)

Gather in a large circle. Say 1 Peter 3:15, 16 together as you display the poster board or chalkboard. Ask the group to think of
times when they need to stand up for their faith as you play the
recording of "I'm Not Ashamed." Close by having each person
say a one-sentence prayer, committing to standing up for his
faith or telling a time when he will stand up for his faith.

Passing Your Faith Along

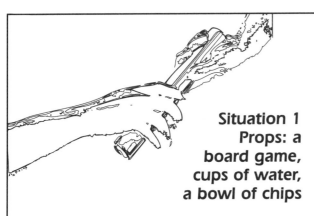

Situation 1
Props: a board game, cups of water, a bowl of chips

Description: A group of you are at a friend's house playing a board game. One of your friends mentions that their new neighbors are Mormons—very friendly, hardworking people. The group discusses some Mormons they've known or who have come to their door. Your friend mentions he might visit their church sometime and check it out. After all, he asserts, churches are no different. How could you look *up, down,* and *out* and stand up for your faith? (Hint: What do you believe about Jesus and the Bible? What do Mormons believe?)

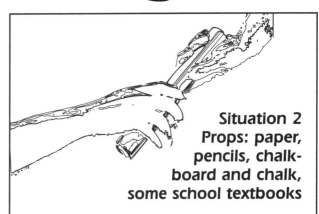

Situation 2
Props: paper, pencils, chalkboard and chalk, some school textbooks

Description: You are at school. Your teacher gives the class the assignment of writing a short paper about George Washington. When you are finished with your paper, the teacher asks for volunteers to read papers to the class. How can you look *up, down,* and *out* and stand up for your faith. (Hint: What have you learned about George Washington's spiritual life and study of Scripture?)

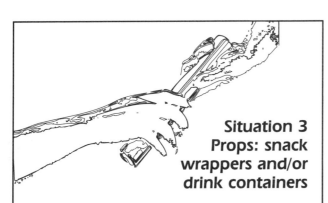

Situation 3
Props: snack wrappers and/or drink containers

Description: You and several friends are out shopping. You stop to get a snack and notice that your friend throws her drinking cup on the ground after she's finished. How can you look *up, down,* and *out* and stand up for your faith? (Hint: What did God entrust us to do with His Creation?)

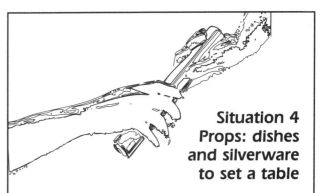

Situation 4
Props: dishes and silverware to set a table

Description: You have several families over for dinner. One of your friends mentions an article he saw in a magazine about another "missing link" that was found for evolution. He laughs because he says he knows you believe all that religious stuff about creation. How can you look *up, down,* and *out* and stand up for your faith? (Hint: Is creation only a "religious" belief?)

Standing Up for _____

GO TEAM!!

Did you know?

A TRACK MEET
TODAY AT 3:00!
BE THERE!

The Bible says...

We believe

Go to Extremes

Truth Relay
Service Projects

Standing up for their faith becomes real to your students when it is acted out in their lives. One way to help them accomplish this goal is to involve them in a service project. Read the suggestions below and choose or adapt one that will work in your community. Challenge your students to stand up for their faith.

Support a Teacher

Have your students order gift subscriptions to *Teachers in Focus* for their teachers, a monthly magazine for teachers published by Focus on the Family. Or call Focus on the Family and inquire about brochures that deal with issues public school teachers face such as lawful ways to teach about God or suggestions for teaching about Thanksgiving.

Clean Up Your Community

Choose an eyesore in your community that students are permitted to clean up. For example, they could clean up trash in a stream or pond, clean up an empty lot, or pick up trash and plant flowers along a street. As students work, take pictures of their efforts. Then work together as a group to write a story for your local newspaper, describing the work and explaining why your class thinks it's important to care for the earth.

A Celebration for Jesus

Have your students plan a party. If possible, choose a place away from the church to have the party, such as a student's house, a park, or a school. Let students choose Christian music to play during the party, make posters that tell about Jesus to decorate for the party, choose snacks and drinks for the party, and choose a Christian video to watch during the party. (Many Christian bookstores have a large selection of Christian videos for rent.)

Encourage students to invite at least three school friends to their party.

Fact Sheets

Photocopy the poster (page 124) that is suggested for the **Bridge the Gap** session. If you have access to a computer, let students work together to design their own page. Photocopy a poster for each of the four topics studied or choose the topic that your students deal with the most. Let students brainstorm the information and the pictures they think should be included with each poster. Students can take pictures with an instant camera to put on the page, if desired. When the students have the information they want, they should neatly print it (or have someone type it) on the page.

Make photocopies of the pages for the students and, if possible, punch holes so the pages will fit in their notebooks. Encourage students to use the fact sheets when they talk to friends or teachers at school.

Donate a Book

Have your students choose several of their favorite books from the ones used during the sessions. Have them participate in a fund-raiser in order to raise money to buy the books. Students can donate the books they buy to their school's library or to your church's library.

Fund-Raising Projects

1. Have a car wash at your building. You can set a price for the wash or simply ask customers for a donation in exchange for a wash. A good time to have the car wash is on a Sunday afternoon after it has been announced in church that morning.

2. Put an announcement in your church bulletin or newsletter that your students are available to do yard work (e.g., weeding, raking, shoveling) on a certain date in exchange for a donation to their project. Schedule times to work at different places throughout the day.

3. Make an arrangement with a group in your church such as a Sunday school class, a weekly Bible study, a choir, or a

teacher's group. Your students will provide snacks and drinks for the group during their meeting and tell briefly about their project so that the group members can make a donation.

4. Let groups in your church know your students are available to help with their meetings and socials for a small donation. Students can wash dishes, vacuum carpets, set up and take down chairs, or pick up trash.